CATHOLIC
FAITH
FOUNDATIONS

BACK TO THE BASICS

DAVID WERNING

Our Sunday Visitor

www.osv.com
Our Sunday Visitor Publishing Division
Our Sunday Visitor, Inc.
Huntington, Indiana 46750

Nihil Obstat
Msgr. Michael Heintz, Ph.D.
Censor Librorum

Imprimatur
✠ Kevin C. Rhoades
Bishop of Fort Wayne-South Bend
December 11, 2017

The *Nihil Obstat* and *Imprimatur* are official declarations that a book is free from doctrinal or moral error. It is not implied that those who have granted the *Nihil Obstat* and *Imprimatur* agree with the contents, opinions, or statements expressed.

Scripture texts in this work are taken from the *New American Bible, revised edition* © 2010, 1991, 1986, 1970 Confraternity of Christian Doctrine, Washington, D.C., and are used by permission of the copyright owner. All rights reserved. No part of the *New American Bible* may be reproduced in any form without permission in writing from the copyright owner.

English translation of the *Catechism of the Catholic Church* for use in the United States of America copyright © 1994, United States Catholic Conference, Inc. — Libreria Editrice Vaticana. English translation of the *Catechism of the Catholic Church: Modifications from the Editio Typica* copyright © 1997, United States Catholic Conference, Inc. — Libreria Editrice Vaticana.

Quotations from papal and other Vatican-generated documents available on vatican.va are copyright © Libreria Editrice Vaticana.

Our Sunday Visitor Publishing Division
Our Sunday Visitor, Inc.
200 Noll Plaza
Huntington, IN 46750
1-800-348-2440

ISBN: 978-1-68192-223-2
(Inventory No. T1928)
eISBN: 978-1-68192-224-9
LCCN: 2017963140

Cover art: Shutterstock
Cover and Interior design: Lindsey Riesen

PRINTED IN THE UNITED STATES OF AMERICA

Contents

FOREWORD

As editor of Our Sunday Visitor Newsweekly, I see up close what topics resonate with our Catholic readers. This resonance is measured in responses to articles and other content via online comment, a letter to the editor, high social media engagement, or a request to share content with a faith community, such as reprinting an article in a parish bulletin.

Without fail, *OSV Newsweekly* consistently receives an overwhelming response when we print content that focuses on the basics of the Faith. So many are thirsting to learn more about the Church's teachings, traditions, and 2,000-year history. Sometimes it's because they are seeking clarity about a specific teaching that they know something about but would like to better understand. Sometimes it's because they want to share a primer on a specific piece of doctrine with a loved one. Sometimes it's because others have asked them: "Why do Catholics …?" and they feel their own response was unsatisfactory. They begin searching for an answer.

The unhappy truth is that, as others have said before, while many Catholics in recent decades have been "sacramentalized," they really haven't been "catechized" or "evangelized." That is, while they may have been baptized, and likely have received the Sacraments of Reconciliation, First Communion, and Confirmation, they never properly learned Church teaching or its rationale on a whole host of issues. Moreover, many Catholics have not been taught how to cultivate a relationship with Jesus Christ — or even that it is important to do so.

Perhaps even more troubling is the perpetuation of a lack of catechesis into the next generation. A couple of years ago, the Center for Applied Research in the Apostolate (CARA) at Georgetown University released a study sponsored by Holy Cross Family Ministries, an organization that promotes family prayer around the world. This study found that only twenty-two percent of Catholic parents go to Mass every Sunday. Of those, only forty-two percent send their children to religious education — meaning that the extent of formal education in faith for the majority of the current young generation who actually attend weekly Mass is only the one hour a week they spend at liturgy. This is far from ideal.

In fact, this problem sparked such a note of concern at the Synods of Bishops on the Family in 2014 and 2015 that Pope Francis chose to devote much of his post-synodal apostolic exhortation, *Amoris Laetitia*, to encouraging increased catechesis for engaged couples, married couples and children (to which he devotes all of the document's Chapter 7).

The harsh truth is that parents are the primary educators of the faith for their children, but they cannot pass on what they do not know. Pope Francis refers to this challenge in *Amoris Laetitia*:

> "Handing on the faith presumes that parents themselves genuinely trust God, seek him and sense their need for him, for only in this way does 'one generation laud your works to another, and declare your mighty acts' (Ps 144:4) and 'fathers make known to children your faithfulness' (Is 38:19). This means that we need to ask God to act in their hearts, in places where we ourselves cannot reach" (287).

In light of these challenges, and rather than wringing our hands at the current state of catechesis, *OSV Newsweekly* identified an opportunity. We determined that we would go back to basics — the basics of the Faith — and offer a series that would be able to respond to the need for more catechesis. To do so, we commissioned a twelve-part series, authored by David Werning, called "Foundations of Faith," which ran once a month in *OSV Newsweekly* throughout 2017. Werning has an S.T.B. in sacred theology from the Catholic University of America. He has been writing about the Church and the Catholic faith since 1992.

The series starts at the very beginning, exploring the Church from her basic foundation of "one, holy, Catholic and apostolic," the "four marks of the Church" given in the Nicene Creed recited each Sunday at Mass. From there, the series presents how God reveals himself through creation, the significance of both Scripture and Tradition, the mystery of the Trinity, what it means to be a member of the Church, the meaning of vocation, morality, and conscience. The final third of the series explores the call to love, what it means to pray, understanding the Communion of the Saints, and an exploration of the four "last things." The results have been compiled in this book, *Catholic Faith Foundations*, and each chapter has received a *nihil obstat*.

This book is appropriate for all people wishing to learn more about the Faith: whether it's those who already are familiar with the Church's teachings, but are in need of a "refresher course," or those who are starting from the beginning.

One other thing to note: While the content is on the "basics" of the Faith, there is serious "meat" to the bones of this book. It gives not only the "what" of the Faith but also the "why" — and it ties it all into a comprehensive understanding of what it means to be Catholic. As one reader said, the series is "an excellent resource for knowledge of our Catholic faith."

For more than one hundred years, Our Sunday Visitor has been a leader in the field of catechesis, giving readers content that helps explain what the Church teaches and why. *Catholic Faith Foundations* is a part of that long legacy. I pray that it brings you closer to Christ.

GRETCHEN R. CROWE
Editor-in-Chief
OSV Newsweekly

PART 1

Shutterstock.com

The Four Marks of the Catholic Church

A Catholic chaplain, a priest, was carrying Communion to patients who were bedridden in a hospital. The priest had a list of Catholic patients who had requested Communion. In one of the rooms, as he blessed a patient and began to leave, the priest was passing by another patient, not on the list, who said, "Hey, what about me?"

The priest stopped and replied, "I'm so sorry; I didn't realize you're a Catholic." The man in the bed said, "I'm not, but what does that matter? Religions are all the same." So the priest said, "In that case, I'm happy to help you become a Catholic. We can start right now." To which the man replied, "No, thank you."

"All religions are the same." The claim is widespread, but when pressed proponents have a difficult time substantiating the claim. Indeed, all one has to do is visit a temple, a mosque, and a church to see how different religions celebrate their beliefs. One can also compare and contrast the

7

various precepts of the religions to learn their differences.

So why do people still make the claim — even those who are practicing a particular religion? Ignorance may be part of the answer. Another part may be a desire to water down all faiths into a one-size-fits-all system that everyone can accept. It may even spring from a well-intentioned effort to alleviate conflict and fighting. The trouble is it doesn't work; there's fighting even among co-religionists.

The fact is all religions are not the same. The challenge is to accept the fact without descending into triumphalism or hostility. A starting point that avoids such confrontations is acknowledging the dignity of the human person and his or her right to religious freedom. This is something the Catholic Church proposes (see *Dignitatis Humanae*, 2).

If people can respect each other as fellow human beings, who deserve the same fundamental rights, then the next step is to move toward mutual understanding through dialogue. A spirit of openness and inquisitiveness about other faiths would be an important part of any meaningful conversation. However, the most important item to bring is a clear understanding of one's own tradition, a prerequisite the Vatican recommends strongly to all Catholics: "Above all they should know their own Church and be able to give an account of its teaching" (*Directory for the Application of Principles and Norms on Ecumenism*, 24).

Catholics can and should feel comfortable speaking openly and knowledgeably about their faith, but too many Catholics feel they don't know (or remember) enough to do so. Only with a firm grasp of the basic foundations of our faith can we help to create a climate in which an informed conversation can take place, avoiding intolerance and ignorance.

This book aims to provide you with a solid understanding of the basic, foundational teachings of the Catholic Church. We will consider key doctrines, Church structure, and Church history, as well as our personal call to growth in holiness. If you've learned it all before but forgotten much of it, this will be a strong refresher course for you. If you're new to the Church or just beginning to learn the teachings of the Faith, this book is an easy-to-follow introduction.

The Catholic Church: Its Basic Foundation

Jesus, during his earthly ministry and before ascending into heaven, instituted his Church upon the "rock" of Peter and the other apostles (see Mt 16:18; 18:18). This Church that Jesus founded subsists in the Catholic Church, according to Catholic teaching, and it still bears the

Key Differences in Major Religions

Core Beliefs

- **Catholics and all other Christians** believe in one God, "the Father and the Son and the Holy Spirit; three persons indeed, but one essence, substance, or nature entirely simple" (*Catechism of the Catholic Church*, 202).
- **Buddhists** have no set conception of a divine being, although Siddhartha Gautama (Buddhism's founder) did speak of gods.
- **Hindus** have a complex idea of divinity involving a divine principle, Brahman, that is manifested by three forms: Vishnu, Shiva, and Brahma.
- **Jews** and **Muslims** are closest to Christianity in that both believe in the one and only God of Abraham. However, they do not accept the Trinity.

Rites and Ceremonies

- **Buddhists** around the world tend to celebrate both the new year and Buddha's birthday. However, the time and manner of celebrations are closely tied to the country and even local area.
- **Hindus** have a ritual called the Vedic sacrifice in which an offering (usually vegetables and grains) is made to appease the gods and bring order to the world.
- The **Jewish** rites include the rite of circumcision for boys (girls are named in a synagogue ceremony on a Sabbath morning within 30 days of their birth) and keeping a complex system of laws, including the dietary laws.
- Like Judaism, **Islam** has a circumcision rite for boys and dietary regulations. Muslims tend to celebrate the transitions in life like marriage and death.

Afterlife

- Regarding the afterlife, **Buddhism** does not have a single vision.
- **Hindus** believe that human beings are reborn over and over again.
- **Muslims** believe in a day of judgment, as well as heaven and hell.
- **Jewish** belief depends on which part of Judaism is under consideration, reminiscent of the debate between the Sadducees and Pharisees, the former rejecting resurrection and the latter accepting. Generally speaking, there is acceptance of some kind of afterlife.

four distinguishing marks that Jesus intended: namely that it is one, holy, catholic, and apostolic. "This Church constituted and organized in the world as a society ... is governed by the successor of Peter and by the bishops in communion with him" (*Lumen Gentium*, 8). The *Catechism* states further, "Only faith can recognize that the Church possesses these properties from her divine source. But their historical manifestations are signs that also speak clearly to human reason" (812).

In order to give an account of their own tradition, Catholics need to understand each of the four marks. Taken together they form a foundation for the entire Catholic faith.

The Church Is One

Claiming that the Catholic Church is one may seem naïve at best and triumphalist at worst. The differences between the Catholic Church and religions outside Christianity are obvious, for the latter do not believe Jesus is God. Within Christianity, the contrasts fall along a spectrum. Quite a few differences stem from both a rejection of the papal office and a disagreement over holy orders. The differences here are very stark. On the other hand, some branches of Christianity, like the Orthodox (which also claims a direct link to apostolic times) are so close that full unity is in reach.

Given these differences within Christianity, and considering the Great Schism of 1054 and the Protestant Reformation in the sixteenth century, how can unity be claimed? It depends on the source of unity. If one keeps in mind the divine origin of the Catholic Church, then its unity can be appreciated even when individual Catholics obscure it by error and sin or when people choose to leave the Church.

The German bishops make a good point: unity is "not a goal of church organization."[1] It is not something that can be manufactured by human beings. The unity of the Church "is already a reality in Christ as a first fruit of the Holy Spirit" (ibid.; see also LG, 7). Therefore, unity is a gift that must be received and lived by the members of the Church, who as Saint Paul tells us are called to be one with their head (cf. Col 1:18).

If one chooses to participate, then he or she will join in the "visible bonds of communion" that Jesus provided:

- "Profession of one faith received from the apostles;

---

1 Stephen Wentworth Arndt, trans., *The Church's Confession of Faith: A Catholic Catechism for Adults*, ed. Mark Jordan (San Francisco: Ignatius, 1987), 231.

Caution about the "One" Church

Two notes of caution about the unity of the Church should be kept in mind. First, unity does not preclude diversity. As the *Catechism* states, "Among the Church's members, there are different gifts, offices, conditions, and ways of life" (814). This includes even the way Mass is celebrated. Most people are familiar with the Latin, or Western, Rite of the Catholic Church, which includes most United States Catholic parishes. But there is an Eastern part, which includes twenty-one churches that celebrate Mass according to their own traditions. Together the Western and Eastern churches make up the one, holy, catholic, and apostolic Church.

A second note of caution concerns Christians outside the Catholic Church. Ruptures to the "unity of Christ's body" (CCC 817) were caused by human sin on the part of both sides of every divide. Yet, "one cannot charge with the sin of the separation those who at present are born into these communities [that resulted from such separation]" (CCC 818). The Catholic Church accepts other Christians as brothers and sisters and recognizes in their churches "elements of sanctification and of truth" (CCC 819). Moreover, the Catholic Church is committed to continual conversion on her part and to responding to Jesus' prayer that all be one in him (Jn 17:20–23).

- Common celebration of divine worship, especially the sacraments;
- Apostolic succession through the Sacrament of Holy Orders."

Participation in these bonds, needless to say, cannot be *pro forma*. They amount to nothing unless love "binds them together in perfect harmony" (CCC 815).

The Church Is Holy

The claim of the Church to be holy may seem false taken at face value. But, again, one has to consider the source to appreciate how the Church is holy. If the Church's holiness depended on her human members, then she would have succumbed to evil long ago. Clearly, individual members and even groups within the Church can be sinful. They may even be actively opposed to holiness. The eruption of scandals throughout the history of the Church, even in the present time, is proof enough. Yet the scandals operate *ipso facto* against the Church's intrinsic holiness.

The Lord says, "Be holy because I [am] holy" (1 Pt 1:16; cf. Lv 11:44, 19:2). We are to reject sin and to live by God's words. So Christ, when he brought the Church into being, did not mean for its members to exist apart from him. On the contrary, the whole point of the Church is to provide a way that people might be united to Jesus and share in all his gifts (cf. 1 Pt 1:13–16). Jesus bestowed the Spirit upon the Church and communicates divine grace through the sacraments. Moreover, the Church has reminded its members that God "does not make men [and women] holy and save them merely as individuals, without bond or link between one another. Rather has it pleased him to bring men together as one people, a people which acknowledges him in truth and serves him in holiness" (LG, 9). The key is to remain in Christ, the source of holiness.

If living a holy life seems impossible to an individual member, then the Church must support that person and remind him or her what Jesus says: "For human beings this is impossible, but for God all things are possible" (Mt 19:26). It's also good to keep in mind models of the Faith, the saints, who persevered in holiness because they never gave in to sin and continued to follow Christ. The saints bring to life the words of Jesus: "I am the vine, you are the branches. Whoever remains in me and I in him will bear much fruit, because without me you can do nothing" (Jn 15:5).

The Church Is Catholic

The third essential characteristic of the Church has become part of her name: catholic, meaning universal. Many people may have heard or read another title: the Roman Catholic Church. However, official Church documents never use "Roman" because it can obscure the universal nature of the Church. Jesus sent the apostles to the whole world (cf. Mt 28:19–20) so that every person might be offered the fruits of his salvation. That's why the Church goes to every land and exists among every people. The Church is even willing to adopt local customs as long as they are good and complement the truth of the Gospel of Christ (cf. LG, 13).

The universality of the Church is enhanced by her presence in so many localities and by her existance within so many political systems across the globe. Every diocese, or local church, makes present the one Catholic Church in its particular place. For instance, just as Paul could write to the "church of God that is in Corinth" (1 Cor 1:2), a person today can write to the "church at Fort Wayne, Indiana," or the

Eastern-Rite Churches

Churches of the Eastern Rite form one of two parts of the Catholic Church. The other part is the Western or Latin-Rite Catholic Church, the mother church of which is in Rome presided over by the pope. The Eastern-Rite Churches have different liturgies, ecclesiastical disciplines, and spiritual heritage, but they all profess the same faith and submit themselves to the authority of the pope. The bishops of all the Churches, east and west, constitute the Apostolic College of Bishops. Many of the Eastern-Rite Churches have counterparts in the Orthodox tradition, which is not in union with Rome and in fact separated from Rome in 1054. Over the years, some of the Orthodox churches reunified with Rome. The Maronite Catholic Church never left communion with Rome. The Eastern Catholic churches have five traditions and twenty-one Churches.

Alexandrian Tradition
• Coptic Catholic Church
• Ethiopian Catholic Church

Antiochene Tradition
• Syro-Malankara Catholic Church
• Maronite Catholic Church
• Syrian Catholic Church

Armenian Tradition
• Armenian Catholic Church

Byzantine Tradition
• Albanian Church
• Belarussian Church
• Bulgarian Catholic Church
• Eparchy of Krizevci
• Greek Catholic Church
• Hungarian Catholic Church
• Italo-Albanian Catholic Church
• Melkite Greek Catholic Church
• Romanian Greek Catholic Church
• Russian Church
• Ruthenian Catholic Church
• Slovak Catholic Church
• Ukrainian Greek Catholic Church

Chaldean Tradition
• Chaldean Catholic Church
• Syro-Malabar Catholic Church

The Orthodox and Catholic churches separated in 1054. With the decline of the Roman Empire, the patriarch of Constantinople thought that the authority over the whole Church should be transferred to his city. The bishop of Rome, however, argued that he was the successor of St. Peter, not Constantinople. In short, they excommunicated each other. Tensions continued so that today the chair of Peter is not recognized to have any authority over the Orthodox. There was also a major disagreement over the inclusion of the world "filioque" ("and the Son") in the creed: the Holy Spirit proceeds from the Father and the Son. The Orthodox interpreted the Latin word as meaning a subordination of the Spirit. Today, both the Orthodox and the Catholic Church have been able to agree on the unity of the Trinity, taking nothing away from any of the divine Persons.

"church at Paris." There are also the Eastern-Rite churches, which bring the variety of their liturgical traditions to the Catholic Church. The fathers at Vatican II were very proud of this richness: the "variety of local churches with one common aspiration is splendid evidence of the catholicity of the undivided Church" (LG, 23).

The Church Is Apostolic

Closely connected to the catholicity of the Church is her apostolic character. Here again one can find people who charge the Church with dissimulation, stating that whatever the Church calls her leaders, she cannot call them apostles. This is true in one sense: The Twelve Apostles chosen by Christ during his earthly ministry, and who received from Christ the great commission to spread the Gospel, are unique. However, the Twelve soon realized that Jesus' promised return was not going to be as quick as they originally thought and, indeed, the Second Coming might happen after their deaths, so they returned to Jesus' words in order to discern how they could fulfill the mission he gave them.

Jesus promised to be with the Church until the end of time through the Holy Spirit, whom the apostles received in a special way at Pentecost. Through prayer the apostles discerned that they were to choose successors to carry the Gospel to the end of time. These successors, who are called bishops today, are not the apostles and they do not claim to be so. What they do claim is to be in the line of apostolic succession that was initiated by the apostles through the laying on of hands. This line of succession is what binds the bishops to hand on the Faith they have received, to guard it and protect it, and to prohibit any innovations obnoxious to it.

Two Ways the Church Is Apostolic

1. Just as the Twelve were given their mission as a body with Peter as the leader, the bishops form a college with the pope as head. As the pope serves his brother bishops as a leader among equals, he shares with them the primary mission of preaching the Gospel of Christ.

2. The whole Church is apostolic in as much as both people and ministers are united in Christ and share in the same mission to make Christ and his kingdom known and available to all.

Conclusion

While other Christian churches celebrate some of the sacraments, revere Sacred Scripture, and have many holy people within their ranks, only the Catholic Church has all the elements Jesus intended:

> This is the one Church of Christ which in the Creed is professed as one, holy, catholic, and apostolic, which our Savior, after his resurrection, commissioned Peter to shepherd, and him and the other apostles to extend and direct with authority, which he erected for all ages as "the pillar and mainstay of the truth." This Church constituted and organized in the world as a society, subsists in the Catholic Church, which is governed by the successor of Peter and by the bishops in communion with him, although many elements of sanctification and of truth are found outside of its visible structure. These elements, as gifts belonging to the Church of Christ, are forces impelling toward catholic unity. (LG, 8)

This teaching, which distinguishes the Catholic Church from other churches, is important for two serious reasons: First, it grounds the teaching and practices of the Catholic Church in the authority of Christ. Second, it warns the Catholic Church never to take for granted her divine gifts, but to work tirelessly to share them with all.

The Salvation of All

Lumen Gentium teaches that the Lord wills that all be saved. The gift is there; people need to receive it. If there is a person who is invincibly ignorant of God's existence and will — i.e., there is no culpability involved — then that person can be saved as long as he or she strives "to live a good life" according to God's grace, which is bestowed upon all:

> "Those also can attain to salvation who, through no fault of their own, do not know the Gospel of Christ or his Church, yet sincerely seek God and, moved by grace, strive by their deeds to do his will as it is known to them through the dictates of conscience. Nor does divine providence deny the help necessary for salvation to those who, without blame on their part, have not yet arrived at an explicit knowledge of God and with his grace strive to live a good life. Whatever good or truth is found amongst them is looked upon by the Church as a preparation for the Gospel. The Church knows that it is given by him who enlightens all men so that they may finally have life. But often men, deceived by the Evil One, have become vain in their reasonings and have exchanged the truth of God for a lie, serving the creature rather than the Creator. Or some there are who, living and dying in this world without God, are exposed to final despair. Wherefore to promote the glory of God and procure the salvation of all of these, and mindful of the command of the Lord, 'Preach the Gospel to every creature,' the Church fosters the missions with care and attention." (16)

The Four Marks of the Catholic Church

STUDY

1. What are the four distinguishing marks of the Catholic Church?
2. What are the three "visible bonds of communion" that Jesus provided?
3. What is the true meaning of the word "catholic"?

CONTEMPLATE

1. How can the Church be holy when its individual members and even groups can be sinful?
2. How can we acknowledge the right to religious freedom for all while still affirming that only the Catholic Church has all the elements Jesus intended?
3. Why is the apostolic character of the Church so important to its mission?

APPLY

1. "Unity does not preclude diversity." How can I appreciate diversity both within the Church and among Christians while still working toward fulfilling Christ's prayer that all be one in him?
2. "Both people and ministers are united in Christ and share in the same mission to make Christ and his kingdom known and available to all." How can I, today, in my ordinary life and work make Christ's kingdom known to those around me?
3. "The key [to holiness] is to remain in Christ, the source of holiness." What is one thing I can do today to become just a tiny bit closer to Christ?

PRAYER

"O God, you who have established the foundations of your Church upon the holy mountains: Grant that she may not be moved by any wiles of error which would fain compass her overthrow, nor may she be shaken by any earthly disquietude, but ever stand firmly upon the ordinances of the Apostles, and by their help, be kept in safety."

— *Pope Saint Leo the Great*

PART 2

God Revealed

In his 1999 letter to artists, Saint John Paul II wrote, "Works of art speak of their authors." One might say the same about God and his work of art: creation. All one has to do is look at the world and the people in it, and one can sense that everything proclaims, "I am wonderfully made" (Ps 139:14).

The Church has taught consistently for more than 2,000 years that God reveals himself through the book of nature, including human beings. Moreover, the *Catechism of the Catholic Church* teaches that God's revelation is communicated gradually. God prepares mankind "to welcome by stages the supernatural Revelation that is to culminate in the person and mission of the incarnate Word, Jesus Christ" (CCC 53). In order to appreciate God's full revelation in Jesus, one needs to appreciate the stages of revelation that lead to him. The stages can be distinguished through the advents of creation, human beings, and the Jewish people.

Pied Beauty by Gerard Manley Hopkins

Glory be to God for dappled things –
    For skies of couple-colour as a brinded cow;
        For rose-moles all in stipple upon trout that swim;
Fresh-firecoal chestnut-falls; finches' wings;
    Landscape plotted and pieced – fold, fallow, and plough;
        And áll trádes, their gear and tackle and trim.

All things counter, original, spare, strange;
    Whatever is fickle, freckled (who knows how?)
        With swift, slow; sweet, sour; adazzle, dim;
He fathers-forth whose beauty is past change:
                    Praise him.

Revelation through Creation

Saint Paul, in the Letter to the Romans, speaks of the first stage of revelation to those who try to suppress the truth of God's existence: "For what can be known about God is evident to them, because God made it evident to them. Ever since the creation of the world, his invisible attributes of eternal power and divinity have been able to be understood and perceived in what he has made" (1:19–20).

The argument has raged ever since. While the Church states matter-of-factly that by "natural reason man can know God with certainty, on the basis of his works" (CCC 50), self-described atheists posit God's nonexistence by appealing to the natural order as well. One of the more popular explanations is the speculation that matter has always existed, and at one point, beyond all probability, some of the matter combined in such a way that made life possible. Still, the question of how matter came into existence remains.

Cardinal Joseph Ratzinger (who later became Pope Benedict XVI) tried to bring the sides together with a philosophical approach that could be accepted by both believer and non-believer. The argument goes like this: everything that exists ipso facto participates in being. Human beings know that they are not the cause of their own being. They also know that many things made by human hands were first thought and then made out of existing matter. But where did the matter come from? Cardinal Ratzinger said that thought precedes matter. Therefore, some being must have thought matter into existence. Christians (among

> ## Wisdom 13:1–9
>
> Foolish by nature were all who were in ignorance of God,
>   and who from the good things seen did not succeed in
> knowing the one who is,
>   and from studying the works did not discern the artisan;
> Instead either fire, or wind, or the swift air,
>   or the circuit of the stars, or the mighty water,
>   or the luminaries of heaven, the governors of the
>   world, they considered gods.
> Now if out of joy in their beauty they thought them gods,
>   let them know how far more excellent is the Lord than these;
>   for the original source of beauty fashioned them.
> Or if they were struck by their might and energy,
>   let them realize from these things how much more powerful
>   is the one who made them.
> For from the greatness and the beauty of created things
>   their original author, by analogy, is seen.
> But yet, for these the blame is less;
> For they have gone astray perhaps,
>   though they seek God and wish to find him.
> For they search busily among his works,
>   but are distracted by what they see, because the things seen are fair.
> But again, not even these are pardonable.
> For if they so far succeeded in knowledge
>   that they could speculate about the world,
>   how did they not more quickly find its Lord?

others) call that being God.[1]

Ratzinger's argument is not a proof in the sense of a scientific proof, but it is a reasonable response to the notion that matter always existed (which, by the way, cannot be proven either). What Ratzinger does want to provide is an entry point for someone who is searching for God. If a person is able to "see" God through creation, he or she may eventually come to faith.

Another approach to exploring God revealed through creation is, appropriately, not logical argument but art and poetry. The Irish Jesuit

---

1 See Part I, Chapter IV of *Introduction to Christianity*, English translation (San Francisco: Ignatius Press, 1990).

poet Gerard Manley Hopkins (1844–1889) sought to articulate the wonder of God present in the beauty of creation in his poem "God's Grandeur":

The world is charged with the grandeur of God
    It will flame out, like shining from shook foil;
    It gathers to a greatness, like the ooze of oil
Crushed. Why do men then now not reck his rod?
Generations have trod, have trod, have trod;
    And all is seared with trade; bleared, smeared with toil;
    And wears man's smudge and shares man's smell; the soil
Is bare now, not can foot feel, being shod.

And for all this, nature is never spent;
    There lives the dearest freshness deep down things;
And though the last lights off the black West went
    Oh, morning, at the brown brink eastward, spring —
Because the Holy Ghost over the bent
    World broods with warm breast and with ah! bright wings."

Aquinas's Five Proofs

Saint Thomas Aquinas is famous for what has been called his five "proofs" of God's existence. But Saint Thomas did not present his words as scientific proof in the present sense of the term. Rather, Aquinas was providing logical arguments that point to the existence of God. The basic conclusion of each is that God is the Uncaused Cause or First Mover. It is also important to keep in mind that Aquinas's five "proofs" in the *Summa Theologiae* (I.Q2.A3) were one part of a grander theological effort. The five "proofs" are:

1. From motion
2. From the nature of the efficient cause
3. From possibility and necessity
4. From the gradation to be found in things
5. From the governance of the world

Revelation through Humans

A second "stage" in God's revelation of himself involves the existence of human beings, who are a part of creation but unique among creatures. The big difference is that man and woman, unlike matter, can ask themselves, "How did I get here?" They know intuitively that their lives and the lives of their ancestors point to some beginning: an endless series of parents and grandparents and so on is not reasonable. Again, something or someone — outside of creation — must have started everything.

The Church teaches that human beings have a kind of deep memory of having been created by God. *Gaudium et Spes*, Vatican II's Pastoral Constitution on the Church in the Modern World, states that from "the very circumstance of his origin man is already invited to converse with God" (19), and the *Catechism* teaches that God invited the first humans "to intimate communion with himself and clothed them with resplendent grace and justice" (54). This deep memory is the very source of humanity's search for meaning and for believers' desire to be reunited with God. But if an individual's existence speaks of God's existence, then why are there some people who do not believe?

What about Evolution?

One question raised by the teaching of God revealed in all of creation is how scientific theories related to evolution and the origins of human life fit in with Catholic doctrine.

One of the most thorough treatments of this question by a pope is found in a 1996 message to the Pontifical Academy of Sciences by Pope Saint John Paul II. Here is an excerpt from his message:

In his encyclical *Humani Generis* (1950), my predecessor Pius XII has already affirmed that there is no conflict between evolution and the doctrine of the faith regarding man and his vocation, provided that we do not lose sight of certain fixed points. ...

And to tell the truth, rather than speaking about the theory of evolution, it is more accurate to speak of the theories of evolution. The use of the plural is required here — in part because of the diversity of explanations regarding the mechanism of evolution, and in part because of the diversity of philosophies involved. There are materialist and reductionist theories, as well as spiritualist theories. Here the final judgment is within the competence of philosophy and, beyond that, of theology.

The magisterium of the Church takes a direct interest in the question of evolution, because it touches on the conception of man, whom Revelation tells us is created in the image and likeness of God. The conciliar constitution Gaudium et Spes has given us a magnificent exposition of this doctrine, which is one of the essential elements of Christian thought. The Council recalled that 'man is the only creature on earth that God wanted for its own sake.' In other words, the human person cannot be subordinated as a means to an end, or as an instrument of either the species or the society; he has a value of his own. He is a person. By this intelligence and his will, he is capable of entering into relationship, of communion, of solidarity, of the gift of himself to others like himself. St. Thomas observed that man's resemblance to God resides especially in his speculative intellect, because his relationship with the object of his knowledge is like God's relationship with his creation. But even beyond that, man is called to enter into a loving relationship with God himself, a relationship which will find its full expression at the end of time, in eternity. Within the mystery of the risen Christ the full grandeur of this vocation is revealed to us. It is by virtue of his eternal soul that the whole person, including his body, possesses such great dignity. Pius XII underlined the essential point: if the origin of the human body comes through living matter which existed previously, the spiritual soul is created directly by God.

As a result, the theories of evolution which, because of the philosophies which inspire them, regard the spirit either as emerging from the forces of living matter, or as a simple epiphenomenon of that matter, are incompatible with the truth about man. They are therefore unable to serve as the basis for the dignity of the human person. (3–5)

The answer is that something went wrong — the Church calls it the first sin, when humanity turned from their Creator in a fruitless effort to become gods themselves. The irony is that because human beings are made in the image and likeness of God, they cannot completely obliterate their connection to him even though they can (and do) make the effort. Nevertheless, most people continue to grope for ultimate meaning and the source of their being. Saint Paul encountered such people when he visited Athens where he sat with and listened to those gathered at the Areopagus. They were searching for the origin of the universe and even posited multiple gods as the source. Paul compliments their intuition and introduces them to God through Jesus Christ. Some of them scoffed and some "became believers" (Acts 17:16–34).

Paul's experience in Athens demonstrates an important limitation to keep in mind about the revelation of God through creation, whether it be physical nature or human: it can bring one to the recognition of a divine being, but it does not necessarily end in knowledge of the God of Judaism and Christianity. To know God personally requires hearing about him from his chosen instruments.

Revelation through Christ

The gathering of the Jewish people into one nation is a third "stage" in God's revelation of himself. After the first sin had alienated humanity from God, God at the opportune time established a relationship with the people of Israel, and they introduced the world to what that relationship means. To summarize greatly the content of the Old Testament, the world comes to know through the Jewish prophets, patriarchs, and people that God is not only the creator but also a loving father: "The Lord, the Lord, a God gracious and merciful, slow to anger and abounding in love and fidelity, continuing his love for a thousand generations" (Ex 34:6–7). God's children, moreover, includes not only the Jewish people, but all people, as God's word to Abraham makes clear: "For I am making you the father of a multitude of nations" (Gn 17:5).

To make the offer of universal salvation unequivocal, God extends his revelation from creation and the Jewish people to one man, Jesus Christ. Through Jesus the revelation of God reaches its fullness, because Jesus demonstrates through his life, death, and resurrection that he is God in the flesh, both truly human and divine.

Jesus gives access to God in a way that builds upon, but far surpasses, the other stages of revelation: "By revealing himself God wishes to make [men and women] capable of responding to him, and of knowing him and of loving him far beyond their own natural capacity" (CCC 52).

The Good News that Jesus came to share with us is that God loves humanity so much that he is willing not only to create the world and charge it with his beauty — including humanity — but also in the face of sin to redeem the world through Jesus and to sustain it through the Holy Spirit. Saint John sums it up well, "For God so loved the world that he gave his only Son, so that everyone who believes in him might not perish but might have eternal life. For God did not send his Son into the world to condemn the world, but that the world might be saved through him" (Jn 3:16–17).

The implications of the Good News are impossible to exhaust. It's not enough to say that human beings can be forgiven through Jesus and, once they have repented, they can live by the grace of the Holy Spirit until they pass into life with God after death. The amazing truth is that God in Jesus has entered the world: God has participated in his creation, even going so far as to become a man. And he does so precisely to invite humanity to participate in the divine being, so as not to be subject to the wages of sin (see Rom 6:23). Since Jesus is both human and divine, he can suffer and die like us, but he is not bound to death like us. When he unites his nature to ours, he orders all things toward eternal life. Even bread and wine become sacraments of redemption. We come "to the Father, through Christ, the Word made flesh, in the Holy Spirit, and thus become sharers in the divine nature" (CCC 51).

"He Is the Beginning"

The famous verses in Colossians (1:15–20), which may have been an early Christian hymn, proclaim that Jesus is the agent not only of creation but also of redemption. Jesus holds together the universe and the Church. He is, indeed, the fullness of God's revelation:

He is the image of the invisible God,
　　the firstborn of all creation.
For in him were created all things in heaven and earth,
　　the visible and the invisible,
　　　　whether thrones or dominions or principalities or powers;
　　all things were created through him and for him.
He is before all things,

> and in him all things hold together.
> He is the head of the body, the church.
> He is the beginning, the firstborn of the dead,
>   that in all things he himself might be preeminent.
> For in him all the fullness was pleased to dwell,
>   and through him to reconcile all things for him,
>   making peace by the blood of his cross
>   [through him], whether those on earth or those in heaven.

God's revelation as it unfolded in time and in different stages brought forth the fullness of his love, incarnated in Jesus. We are invited to share in God's love by immersing ourselves in Christ, which begins by hearing his word and then keeping it (see Lk 11:28). Jesus has provided the means through the sacraments and promises to abide with us through his Holy Spirit. As we unite ourselves to him, we not only discover the source of everything but also find the person God intended us to be. The key is to abide in God's revelation, for the Lord has made known his loving plan to bring all mankind to him.

Pope Saint John Paul II on the Revelation of Christ

"Man cannot live without love. He remains a being that is incomprehensible for himself, his life is senseless, if love is not revealed to him, if he does not encounter love, if he does not experience it and make it his own, if he does not participate intimately in it. This, as has already been said, is why Christ the Redeemer 'fully reveals man to himself.' If we may use the expression, this is the human dimension of the mystery of the Redemption. In this dimension man finds again the greatness, dignity and value that belong to his humanity. In the mystery of the Redemption man becomes newly 'expressed' and, in a way, is newly created. He is newly created! 'There is neither Jew nor Greek, there is neither slave nor free, there is neither male nor female; for you are all one in Christ Jesus.' The man who wishes to understand himself thoroughly — and not just in accordance with immediate, partial, often superficial, and even illusory standards and measures of his being — he must with his unrest, uncertainty and even his weakness and sinfulness, with his life and death, draw near to Christ. He must, so to speak, enter into him with all his own self, he must 'appropriate' and assimilate the whole of the reality of the Incarnation and Redemption in order to find himself. If this profound process takes place within him, he then bears fruit not only of adoration of God but also of deep wonder at himself. How precious must man be in the eyes of the Creator, if he 'gained so great a Redeemer,' and if God 'gave his only Son' in order that man 'should not perish but have eternal life.'" — *Redemptor Hominis*, 10

God Revealed

STUDY

1. What are the three "stages of revelation" that lead to God?
2. How do scientific theories like evolution fit with Catholic teaching?
3. In what way does the revelation of God reach its fullness in Jesus?

CONTEMPLATE

1. Pope Saint John Paul II says that "man cannot live without love." What happens if someone tries to live without love?
2. When Jesus unites his nature to ours, he orders all things toward eternal life. What does being ordered toward eternal life look like to you?
3. In what ways does an eternal soul give a human body its essential dignity?

APPLY

1. One approach to exploring God as revealed through creation is through art and poetry. Even if you don't consider yourself an artist, how can you use art to express the wonder of God?
2. "The Church teaches that human beings have a kind of deep memory of having been created by God." What "deep memory" of being created have you experienced? How can you use this memory to increase your love of God?
3. "We are invited to share in God's love by immersing ourselves in Christ." What is one way you can immerse yourself in Christ today?

PRAYER

O merciful God, grant that I may ever perfectly
do Your will in all things.

Let it be my ambition to work only for Your honor
and glory.

Let me rejoice in nothing but what leads to You,
nor grieve for anything

that leads away from You.

May all passing things be as nothing in my eyes,
and may all that is Yours

be dear to me, and You, my God, dear above them
all.

May all joy be meaningless without You, and may
I desire nothing apart from You.

May all labor and toil delight me when it is for
You.

— *Saint Thomas Aquinas*

Renata Sedmakova / Shutterstock.com

PART 3

Scripture and Tradition

The Catholic Church has proclaimed from its beginning that the Christian faith is handed on through both sacred Tradition and sacred Scripture. Some Christian traditions maintain that all revealed truth is handed on through Scripture alone (*sola scriptura*). The Catholic Church, in contrast, has always maintained that the one wellspring of divine revelation is communicated through two fonts: sacred Tradition and sacred Scripture. The Church notes that, before there were written Scriptures, the Christian community (and the Jewish community, too) handed on God's word through preaching.

Saint Paul wrote to the Thessalonians saying, "Stand firm and hold fast to the traditions that you were taught, either by an oral statement or by a letter of ours" (2 Thes 2:15). Implicit in Paul's words (and something he reminds people often) is the authority he has as an apostle to hand on the authentic teaching about Jesus and the Church.

Today the Church continues Paul's service through its teaching office, the Magisterium. The Magisterium is a gift that has as its main purpose to protect the deposit of faith which has been handed on through sacred Tradition and sacred Scripture. One can imagine the confusion which would result in a community without such a teaching authority. To appreciate its function, however, one must be clear about how the Church defines sacred Tradition and sacred Scripture.

By "Tradition," the Catholic Church means all that the apostles handed on from their experience of Jesus and from what they learned by the inspiration of the Holy Spirit. This includes their rich Jewish heritage and the blessings they received as they practiced their faith in Jesus after he had ascended into heaven (see *Catechism of the Catholic Church*, 83).

Obviously the Gospels and the other parts of the New Testament were not written until after the events of Jesus' life. The apostles on their missionary journeys would hand on orally the content of the Faith: the words and deeds of Jesus, his interpretation of the Hebrew Scriptures, the signs he performed, etc. Moreover, the Faith was not only proclaimed but also celebrated when the people gathered together in the breaking of the bread (what we call the Mass). When there were disagreements, the apostles met in the Holy Spirit to resolve them. The Council of Jerusalem was the first such meeting, at which the question of how gentile converts became members of the Church was posed and answered (see Acts 15).

The Early Church

Very soon it became evident that Jesus was not going to return as quickly as the early Church thought, so the evangelists and the other authors of the New Testament decided to put into writing all that they had witnessed and learned. Obviously, though the modes of transmission differed, the content remained inspired. In order to resolve conflicts concerning authentic content, the early Church would meet and pray to the Holy Spirit for a resolution as it did at the Jerusalem Council. In fact, the apostles established the office of bishop precisely to protect the deposit of faith, which led to the Magisterium, as we shall see after considering sacred Scripture.

It's important to keep in mind that, for the original followers of Jesus, Scripture was what we now refer to as the Hebrew Bible or the Old Testament, which came about in much the same way as the New Testament: the Israelite community put down in writing for future generations what it received from the Lord. For the early Church, there was no New Testament in writing — everything was passed on by word of mouth. Thus, the Church sees the Gospels coming about in three distinct stages: the life and teaching of Jesus, the oral tradition, and the written Gospels themselves. It's possible that as the New Testament was being written, the writers had a sense that they were complementing the books of their Jewish ancestors. They did know that they were putting into writing what they had received from the apostles and their successors. Certainly the content of the New Testament manifests the authors' Spirit-driven work to share the good news of Jesus Christ.

Moreover, the Church is confident in declaring the divine origin of the Scriptures (both Hebrew and Christian): "In composing the sacred books, God chose men and while employed by him they made use of their powers and abilities ... [to write] everything and only those things which he wanted. Therefore ... the books of Scripture ... [teach] solidly, faithfully, and without error that truth which God wanted put into sacred writings for the sake of salvation" (*Dei Verbum*, 11).

When the Church says that Scripture teaches "without error" what God wanted his people to know for the sake of their salvation, it is respecting the intent of the authors (including the Lord himself, who is the Author behind the authors, so to speak) and what they wanted to convey. For example, when Isaiah writes "All flesh is grass" (Is 40:6), he does not mean that human skin is grass; he is expressing the truth of human mortality. God uses human language and human authors to carry his truth to us (just like he took on human nature to save us). This includes different kinds of literature — poems, short stories, histories, myths, parables, Gospels, letters, encomiums — and different writers to express his truth. A reader has to be aware of what he or she is reading to be able to appreciate what God is saying.

Inspired Texts

When we approach the Scriptures, therefore, we should do so with great reverence. This is true for all Scripture. As Christians we understand the New Testament as fulfilling the Old, but this does not mean that the Old Testament is less important or lacking divine inspiration. Quite the contrary, the Church believes that the Old Testament foreshadows and anticipates the coming of Christ. Therefore, we read the Scriptures as a whole; both testaments shed light on each other.

We also read the Scriptures in relationship with the Church, which brings us back to Jesus, who is the head of the Church. If Jesus is the fullness of revelation, then there is no more revelation to be received.

The Canon of Scripture

Over time, the Church began to define more clearly the divine authorship of the biblical texts and put them into a canon, or a list of writings determined to be inspired by the Holy Spirit. This canon was basically fixed by the fourth century but was defined infallibly only in the sixteenth century at the Council of Trent. The Catholic Church teaches that the canon of sacred Scripture includes seventy-three books: forty-six books for the Old Testament and twenty-seven for the New.

Books of the Bible

The Old Testament:

Genesis	Song of Songs	
Exodus	Wisdom	
Leviticus	Sirach	
Numbers	Isaiah	
Deuteronomy	Jeremiah	
Joshua	Lamentations	
Judges	Baruch	
Ruth	Ezekiel	
1 and 2 Samuel	Daniel	
1 and 2 Kings	Hosea	
1 and 2 Chronicles	Joel	
Ezra	Amos	
Nehemiah	Obadiah	
Tobit	Jonah	
Judith	Micah	
Esther	Nahum	
1 and 2 Maccabees	Habakkuk	
Job	Zephaniah	
Psalms	Haggai	
Proverbs	Zechariah	
Ecclesiastes	Malachi	

The New Testament:

Matthew
Mark
Luke
John
Acts of the Apostles
Romans
1 and 2 Corinthians
Galatians
Ephesians
Philippians
Colossians
1 and 2 Thessalonians
1 and 2 Timothy
Titus
Philemon
Hebrews
James
1 and 2 Peter
1, 2 and 3 John
Jude
Revelation (the Apocalypse)

Some non-Catholic Christian denominations do not accept all seventy-three books. The ones in question are what have come to be called the deutero-canonical books: Judith, Tobit, Wisdom, Ecclesiasticus (Sirach), Baruch, 1 and 2 Maccabees, and parts of Daniel and Esther.

Everything we need to know about God, about his will, and about salvation has been made known to us by Jesus. However, recognizing the need to correct errors and combat confusion, the apostles established the office of bishop to carry on the duty of teaching and to protect the deposit of faith they had received from Jesus.

Revelation, therefore, is intrinsically bound with apostolic succession. When Jesus sent the Holy Spirit on the apostles at Pentecost, he established their teaching authority. The gift of the Holy Spirit kept them from error in matters necessary for the salvation of the faithful. The apostles in turn passed on this charism (through the laying on of hands) to the bishops and their successors (priests and deacons share in the bishop's authority vicariously).

The Magisterium

The Magisterium is the teaching authority of the Church. The pope (or bishop of Rome) and the bishops in union with him form the Magisterium. Its main task is to authentically interpret God's word, whether written or handed on orally. The Magisterium prepares for its task by meditating on Scripture and Tradition and by praying continually for God's guidance. The Magisterium is a true gift to the people of God, because it protects Revelation from relativism.

Dei Verbum, the 1965 Dogmatic Constitution on Divine Revelation, offers the following insight into the Magisterium of the Catholic Church:

> The task of authentically interpreting the word of God, whether written or handed on, has been entrusted exclusively to the living teaching office of the Church, whose authority is exercised in the name of Jesus Christ. This teaching office is not above the word of God, but serves it, teaching only what has been handed on, listening to it devoutly, guarding it scrupulously, and explaining it faithfully in accord with a divine commission and with the help of the Holy Spirit, it draws from this one deposit of faith everything which it presents for belief as divinely revealed.

> It is clear, therefore, that sacred Tradition, sacred Scripture, and the teaching authority of the Church, in accord with God's most wise design, are so linked and joined together that one cannot stand without the others, and that all together and each in its own way under the action of the one Holy Spirit contribute effectively to the salvation of souls. (10)

Throughout the Church's existence, the Magisterium has corrected errors and defined truths. For example, the teaching office came to the aid of all believers by defining, after first appealing to Scripture and Tradition, that Jesus is both divine and human. We may have difficulty understanding this truth, but the Magisterium defined it because so many people were arguing about it.

Therefore, when we approach Scripture or a teaching from the Magisterium, we do so as members of the Church, members of the Body of Christ. We do not come to the Bible or Tradition as mere individuals. We have our individual minds, of course, and we certainly can question and ponder and test what we receive. However, we should adopt a spirit of openness to the Holy Spirit's grace that has so evidently worked through the Church.

Church Authority

The Church, for its part, gives guidance to the people of God by assigning different levels of authority to documents and teachings. Scripture, of course, has been defined as God's revelation in written form (and coming out of Tradition), so the truths conveyed through Scripture deserve our full assent. On the other hand, the Magisterium is able to guide the Church to a deeper understanding of Scripture as it yields to the Holy Spirit.

The Magisterium comes to the aid of Church members by assigning different levels of authority to particular documents and teachings. A statement delivered and defined *ex cathedra* (i.e., with the full authority of his office) by the pope, or a document released by all the bishops together (including the pope), has the highest authority. The Magisterium's authority, at whatever level it is exercised, extends over faith and morals, what members of the Church need to know for salvation. If a pope or a bishop expresses an opinion on the weather or a political campaign, or any subject clearly outside his role as teacher of the Faith, then we can take it or leave it.

If a pope or a bishop expresses an opinion on a sports team or a favorite food, or any subject clearly outside his role as teacher of the faith, then we can take it or leave it.

The pope has a number of ways to express his authority as the vicar of Christ. There is the apostolic constitution that solemnly announces a papal teaching on a doctrinal or disciplinary question. A papal bull may also be used as a dramatic way to present a solemn pronouncement. The pope might also release an encyclical, which is a letter explaining more clearly a doctrine or serious pastoral issue within the Church. Although not as solemn as the former two, it deserves the respect of the entire Church.

"Doctrine" refers to a teaching of the Church regarding faith and morals. "Dogma" refers to doctrines that have been explicitly defined by the magisterium; they are truths contained in sacred Tradition and/or sacred Scripture that oblige everyone in the Church to an irrevocable commitment of faith (for example, the divinity of Christ or the real presence of Jesus' body and blood in the Eucharist).

Goal of Salvation

Whether a teaching is explicitly mentioned in Scripture or not, the Magisterium at times finds it appropriate to offer certain definitions. Dogmas, for example, are teachings that the Magisterium declares are part of the deposit of faith (again, for example, the two natures of Christ). Other teachings, like the content of the Bible, which was defined at the Council of Trent, do not rise to the level of dogma but are clearly important to the life of the Church and so come under the teaching authority of the Magisterium.

The important thing to remember is that the goal of both sacred Tradition and sacred Scripture is our salvation. God reveals himself to us so that we remain united to him forever. He therefore provides us with the means to enter into relationship with him, not merely as individuals but as brothers and sisters in Christ, who remains the fullness of revelation. Scripture and Tradition, along with the teaching authority of the Magisterium, are divine aids to help us put on the mind of Christ and journey with him, in the Spirit, to the Father.

Reading and Understanding Sacred Scripture

Senses of Scripture

In order to help the faithful appreciate the truth conveyed by Scripture, the Magisterium provides a number of "senses" to keep in mind when one is reading the Bible (see CCC 115–119).

• **Literal Sense:** First, we need to pick up the book and read it and simply ask: What is it saying? Who did what? When? Where? Why? Am I reading a poem or a letter or something else? This is reading and interpreting Scripture in the way the author intended to communicate. Some readers use colored markers to clarify which pronoun refers to which person, for example. Consulting biblical resources like the *Catechism* or a concordance can also be very helpful. But until this level is completed, one cannot progress to deeper meanings that certainly are contained in Scripture.

• **Allegorical Sense:** Step two is to reflect on what we have read. What does the text mean? More importantly for us as Christians, what does the text mean in the light of Christ? We should also be attentive to what the Church has taught about the text in question.

• **Moral Sense:** After reading and reflecting, we need to react. How is my life affected by what I have read? Am I adopting a sacrificial love that leads me to place God and other persons before myself, just as Jesus did for me? How do I need to change my life in order to become more Christ-like? "Blessed are those who hear the word of God and observe it" (Lk 11:28).

• **Anagogical Sense:** Finally, there is the mystical or anagogical sense of Scripture, which means being led up or to rise. How is my reading, reflecting, and reacting leading me to a deeper and more intimate relationship with God?

— STUDY GUIDE PART 3 ———————————————

Scripture and Tradition

STUDY

1. What does the Church mean by "sacred Tradition"?
2. Why was the office of bishop established?
3. What is the difference between doctrine and dogma?

CONTEMPLATE

1. The Church says that Scripture teaches "without error" what God wants his people to know. What does "without error" mean to you? How can you explain it to someone who points out "mistakes" in the Bible?
2. What is more important in your faith life: sacred Scripture or sacred Tradition? If there is an imbalance, how can you correct it?
3. Why is it important to interpret Scripture as a member of the Church and not as an individual?

APPLY

1. Reading Scripture is an excellent way to get to know the will of God. Select one book of the Bible and begin reading it prayerfully over the next week.
2. The early Church met and prayed to the Holy Spirit when in need of wisdom. What is one area of your life where you can invite the Holy Spirit to enlighten you?
3. We are to approach the Scriptures with reverence. What can you do to increase your knowledge and love of both the Old and New Testaments?

PRAYER

Let me not, O Lord, be puffed up with worldly wisdom, which passes away, but grant me that love which never abates, that I may not choose to know anything among men but Jesus, and him crucified.

I pray thee, loving Jesus that as thou hast graciously given me to drink in with delight the words of thy knowledge, so thou would mercifully grant me to attain one day to thee, the fountain of all wisdom and to appear forever before thy face. Amen.

— *Saint Bede*

The Trinity: Central Mystery of Our Faith

No matter how one puts it, the Christian belief in the Holy Trinity is a difficult teaching to get one's mind around. The Athanasian Creed, written around the fourth or fifth century, puts it this way: "We worship one God in Trinity and Trinity in Unity, neither confounding the persons nor dividing the substance." How can God be one divine substance and at the same time three distinct persons? It's not one God appearing as Father or Son or Spirit at separate moments. Each one is who he is, and yet there remains one God.

In order to protect the teaching of the Trinity that it had received from sacred Tradition and sacred Scripture, the Church had to defeat a number of heresies during the first few centuries following the life of Christ.

Arianism and Macedonianism were rejected, for they failed to admit the co-equality and co-eternity of the Persons who are God. Sabellianism and other kinds of Modalism were rejected, for they held that there are not really three distinct Persons, but only One.… … Also rejected were rationalistic theories that were really tritheisms, holding that there are three divine substances or gods rather than only one divine wisdom and love, in which three Persons subsist, who are one God.[1]

The Athanasian Creed, written around the fourth or fifth century, puts the Church's teaching this way: "We worship one God in Trinity and Trinity in Unity, neither confounding the Persons nor dividing the substance."

Experience the Trinity

Perhaps one way to approach the mystery of the Trinity is to avoid putting too much emphasis on explanations and place more emphasis on experience. This is not to suggest a retreat from the rational, but rather to affirm that all human experience — including faith experience — can contribute to our knowledge as well.

There have been many attempts to try to explain the Trinity, the most famous attributed to St. Patrick. Evidently, St. Patrick tried to show how a shamrock, which is a single plant with three leaves, is analogous to the one triune God with three distinct persons. Others have used water, which is always H_2O but can be a liquid, ice or steam. Still others speak about one woman being at the same time mother, daughter and sister. Ultimately, each example falls short of the Church's belief in the Trinity because, while each shows how something can have "oneness" and "threeness" at the same time, none of them capture the truth of the Trinity. For God is not made up of parts, and he does not exist in different modes or forms. He is Father, Son and Spirit: three distinct persons, but one divine substance.

For example, how would you like to be explained? A panel of experts consisting of a physiologist, a psychologist, and a spiritual master could be convened to determine once and for all who you are. At the end of

---

1 Cardinal Donald Wuerl, Ronald Lawler, and Thomas Comerford Lawler, eds. *The Teaching of Christ: A Catholic Catechism for Adults*, 4th ed. (Huntington, IN: Our Sunday Visitor, Inc., 1995).

a three-year study, the panel could issue an exhaustive report with bar graphs, pie charts, and statistics, detailing everything about you down to your biochemical make-up. A news conference would be called and a panel of distinguished experts would announce with absolute certainty: this is John (or Jane); nothing more can be known about him (or her).

The very idea of being able to explain fully an individual human being is, of course, ridiculous. Having a complete list of facts about someone — even if it is possible to compile — does not lead to a complete understanding of the person at his or her depths. At best, such a list provides a "snapshot" of the person at a certain moment in time. Interesting facts? Yes. A full revelation of the human person? No.

The truth is this: each human being is a mystery who can never be explained fully. And yet, at the same time, each human being can be known in a deep and real way if one is willing to enter into a close relationship with that person.

The same is true for coming to know the Holy Trinity. The Trinity defies explanation. Even to know the existence of the Trinity required a revelation, which was provided by Jesus. The clearest example is what has come to be known as the Great Commission, which the resurrected Lord spoke to his apostles just prior to ascending to heaven: "Go, therefore, and make disciples of all nations, baptizing them in the name of the Father, and of the Son, and of the Holy Spirit, teaching them to observe all that I have commanded you. And behold, I am with you always, until the end of the age" (Mt 28:19–20).

The apostles received the words of Jesus, and his deeds, not as bits of data to analyze, but as the revelation of God to act upon. In doing so, they began to build up the Church that Jesus intended to establish: a community of persons who, through Jesus, may participate in the communion of the Trinity. This experience does not preclude the Church from trying to understand Jesus' words or from examining them with the lens of theology. But it includes more. Our relationship with Jesus, as individuals and as a Church, makes it possible to come to know the Trinity.

Revealed by the Son

Through his incarnation, and eventually through his public ministry, Jesus revealed (by word and deed) not only humanity to itself, but also God to humanity. Indeed, the fact that Jesus would often make declarative statements about God is what brought him into such great disfavor with many of the religious leaders at the time. Nevertheless, many others — having heard Jesus speak and witnessed his amazing signs — believed in him and became his disciples. By yielding to Jesus and being open to his Gospel, the disciples were brought to a deeper understanding of the inner life of God, and years later, when the Church was in its beginning stages, they passed on what they had received.

One of the first things revealed by Jesus concerns God the Father, which may seem odd to anyone familiar with the Jewish faith. Why would Jesus have to reveal the Father to the Jewish people? They were already aware of God as a father and a protector through the preaching of the prophets and through the experience of having been made a nation by God. They took for granted that God the Father had created everything, that he had led Israel to the promised land, and, indeed, that he would always care for them. God the Father was already well known to the Jewish people.

But Jesus reveals something new: God is not only a father to the Jewish people; he is father to Jesus in a unique and exclusive way. Jesus is well known for referring to God as Father, but he also says repeatedly that he was sent by the Father (cf. Jn 8:29; 17:18; 20:21). Moreover, Jesus claims a special relationship: "All things have been handed over to me by my Father. No one knows the Son except the Father, and no one knows the Father except the Son and anyone to whom the Son wishes to reveal him" (Mt 11:27; see also Jn 14:7). Finally, Jesus reveals that the special relationship he enjoys with the Father discloses a previously unknown truth: "The Father and I are one" (Jn 10:30).

If Jesus had said nothing else, then the Church would have had to discern only what he meant by his references to the Father. However,

"To believe in the Trinity is to believe that there is only one God, and that there are three distinct Persons who possess eternally the same divine nature. To say that there is only one God or only one divine nature is to say that there is no plurality of divine beings. Thus there is only one Wisdom, one Love, one Life that is God, the source and goal of all. The one only God exists in three Persons, the Father, the Son, and the Holy Spirit, three who are distinct, but who know us with one infinite wisdom and who love us with one eternal love, and with whom we can enter into personal relationships through grace."

— Cardinal Donald Wuerl, Ronald Lawler, and Thomas Comerford Lawler, eds. *The Teaching of Christ: A Catholic Catechism for Adults,* 4th ed. (Huntington, IN: Our Sunday Visitor, Inc., 1995).

as has already been noted, Jesus tells his disciples to baptize people in the name of the Father and of the Son and of the Holy Spirit. He also reassures his disciples that he will be with them always through "the Spirit of truth" (Jn 14:16–17), the same Spirit who remained with Jesus throughout his ministry (Jn 1:29–34) and who would be given to the Church at Pentecost by both Father and Son. Indeed, the Spirit is the presence of God at work in the Church, leading all the members toward the fulfillment of the divine will which ends in eternal life. The references to the Holy Spirit, therefore, disclose another truth about the inner life of God, namely that God is a unity of three Persons. Those who are baptized according to Jesus' instruction share not only in the gift of the Holy Spirit but also in the Trinitarian communion.

Words for Love

When considering the inner life of God, it is important to remember that whatever can be said is the fruit of prayerful discernment on the part of the Church for hundreds of years. Moreover, what has been said is articulated in words that have been used to help explain the mystery of the Trinity. The original disciples would most likely scratch their heads if someone mentioned the word "trinity" to them. Even the word "person" is used in a highly technical sense that is distinguished from its application to human beings. When used of God, "person" is intended to denote the distinctions within the Godhead. Based on Jesus' ministry and the experience of the apostles, the Church gradually described God in this way: "It is the Father who generates, the Son who is begotten, and the Holy Spirit who proceeds" (CCC 254). The language is meant to help the Church grow in understanding of God's interaction with the world, even though it is impossible to exhaust the mystery of God.

While the present age has benefited from the prayer and thought of the Church in years past when it comes to appreciation of the Trinity, no time period has ever been without the eternal witness of Jesus, whose words and deeds remain potent and active in the lives of his disciples. Jesus did not use technical theological language, but rather stories and parables that expressed the truth in a more immediate way. When he spoke about the Father and Spirit, he always used relational terms that underscored the essential Trinitarian truth: God is love. Indeed, it finally dawned upon the Church as it discerned the Gospel that the essential meaning of the Trinity is an outpouring of love that gives birth to creation and that extends the offer of eternal life to all mankind.

The belief in the Holy Trinity did not come about through abstract thought or the collection of data, even though the Church did eventually develop a formal doctrine. The Trinity was revealed long before it was part of a catechism. As the members of the Church made the effort to receive well the Gospel of Christ, and to love each other, they began to experience on a deep level the union Jesus promised, which bore fruit in the spreading of the Faith and the sharing of life with God.

The Trinity at Mass

A venerable principle of Catholic teaching is "*Lex Orandi, Lex Credendi*," which means that the Church prays what it believes. When the community gathers at Mass, they are not participating in an empty ritual, but in a real communion of love that is celebrated. Priest and people, united in Christ, through the power of the Holy Spirit, offer worship to the Father. Consider the preface to the liturgy of the Eucharist for the Mass of the Most Holy Trinity:

It is truly right and just, our duty and our salvation,
always and everywhere to give you thanks,
Lord, holy Father, almighty and eternal God.
For with your Only Begotten Son and the Holy Spirit
you are one God, one Lord:
not in the unity of a single person,
but in a Trinity of one substance.
For what you have revealed to us of your glory
we believe equally of your Son
and of the Holy Spirit,
so that, in the confessing of the true and eternal Godhead,
you might be adored in what is proper to each Person,
their unity in substance,
and their equality in majesty.
For this is praised by Angels and Archangels,
Cherubim, too, and Seraphim,
who never cease to cry out each day,
as with one voice they acclaim:
Holy, Holy, Holy Lord God of hosts....
— *The Roman Missal*

One of those fruits is how the truth of the Trinity is reflected in the human family. "The word of God tells us that the family is entrusted to a man, a woman, and their children, so that they may become a communion of persons in the image of the union of the Father, the Son and the Holy Spirit. Begetting and raising children, for its part, mirrors God's creative work" (*Amoris Laetitia*, 29). Just as the communion of Father, Son, and Spirit give life, the family is called to do so as well. And not just in the obvious way of having children, as grand a blessing as this may be. The family also gives life when they work together, enjoy each other's company, forgive, pray, and even play together. Moreover, a family is able to reflect God's love when it contributes to the common good through charitable service. In short, the family mirrors the Trinity best when it truly lives in the Spirit of Christ.

The best way for anyone to come to a knowledge of the reality of the Holy Trinity is to act upon the words and deeds of Christ: "Whoever loves me will keep my word, and my Father will love him, and we will come to him and make our dwelling with him.... The Advocate, the holy Spirit that the Father will send in my name — he will teach you everything and remind you of all that [I] told you" (Jn 14:23, 26).

"[The] confession of the triune God is a deep mystery that no created spirit can discover of itself or ever comprehend. It is the mystery of an unfathomable and overflowing love: God is not a solitary being, but a God who bestows and communicates himself out of the abundance of his being, a God who lives in the communion of Father, Son, and Spirit, and who can therefore also bestow and ground community. Because he is life and love in himself, God is able to be life and love for us. We are included from all eternity in the mystery of God. From all eternity God has a place for us. The confession of the triune God is ultimately an exposition of the single sentence "God is love" (1 Jn 4:8, 16b). God in himself is life and love from all eternity, so that he grounds hope for us in the midst of a world of death and hate. We should know in faith that the ultimate and deepest reality is life and love and that a share in this reality is bestowed on us through Jesus Christ in the Holy Spirit."

— Stephen Wentworth Arndt, trans., and Mark Jordan, ed., *The Church's Confession of Faith: A Catholic Catechism for Adults* (San Francisco: Ignatius, 1987).

Living This Truth

As an institution, the Church has never ceased to live its Trinitarian faith. Every new Christian is initiated through baptism, the prayers of which call upon the Trinity to free the newly baptized from sin and to bring him or her into the communion with the head, Jesus, and his members, the people of God. Every celebration of the Eucharist, moreover, begins and ends with the Sign of the Cross, which signifies the assembly's participation in the life of the Trinity.

To return to the example of coming to know a fellow human being: we do so by spending time with the person, by talking and listening and sharing experiences. The person is known more or less deeply depending on the quantity and quality of time shared. Our faith tells us that God wants to be known in a similar way, which is why Jesus became incarnate. As a human being, Jesus can be known by us; we can enter a relationship with him. We can read his words, meditate on his deeds, imitate his life. And as a member of the Trinity, Jesus can unite us to himself so that we partake in the communion of love, which bears the fruit of peace and trust, giving us the grace to anticipate the life of heaven even now.

So, while it may be true that no one can fully explain the Trinity, it is possible to invite others to experience the Trinity through the way one participates in the love of Father, Son, and Spirit.

Batter My Heart, Three-Person'd God

by John Donne
Batter my heart, three-person'd God, for you
As yet but knock, breathe, shine, and seek to mend;
That I may rise and stand, o'er throw me, and bend
Your force to break, blow, burn, and make me new.
I, like an usurp'd town to another due,
Labor to admit you, but oh, to no end;
Reason, your viceroy in me, me should defend,
But is captiv'd, and proves weak or untrue.
Yet dearly I love you, and would be lov'd fain,
But am betroth'd unto your enemy;
Divorce me, untie or break that knot again,
Take me to you, imprison me, for I,
Except you enthrall me, never shall be free,
Nor ever chaste, except you ravish me.

— STUDY GUIDE PART 4 —————————————————

The Trinity: Central Mystery of Our Faith

STUDY

1. What is the Trinity?
2. What did Jesus reveal about God the Father?
3. What is the role of the Holy Spirit in the Church today?

CONTEMPLATE

1. "It is the Father who generates, the Son who is begotten, and the Holy Spirit who proceeds" (*Catechism of the Catholic Church*, 254). What do the words "generates," "is begotten," and "proceeds" mean to you and your faith?
2. Do you pray differently when you pray to the Father? To the Son? To the Holy Spirit? If so, what is the difference?
3. What words would you use to describe the Trinity to your friends and family?

APPLY

1. Jesus tells all of us to go forth and make disciples of all nations. What can you do, in your life as it is now, to fulfill this Great Commission?
2. A relationship with Jesus helps us understand the Trinity. How can you deepen your understanding of the Trinity by working on your relationship with Jesus this week?
3. The essential Trinitarian truth is God is love. What is one concrete way you can share the love of God with someone today?

PRAYER

Eternal God, eternal Trinity, you have made the blood of Christ so precious through his sharing in your divine nature. You are a mystery as deep as the sea; the more I search, the more I find, and the more I find the more I search for you. But I can never be satisfied; what I receive will ever leave me desiring more. When you fill my soul I have an even greater hunger, and I grow more famished for your light. I desire above all to see you, the true light, as you really are.

— *Saint Catherine of Siena*

Spencer Grant

Belonging to the Church

"**A**re you a member of the Catholic Church?" The answer to this question must be obvious to a lot of people. According to Georgetown University's Center for Applied Research in the Apostolate (CARA), more than seventy-four million persons in the United States self-identified as Catholics in 2016. That means if the U.S. population was 325 million in the same year, then twenty-three percent said, "Yes, I am a Catholic," and seventy-seven percent said, "No, I am not."[1] Simple, right?

Actually, it's not that simple. CARA also found that a little more than three-fourths of the seventy-four million self-identified Catholics said they did not attend Mass each week. Now that's a problem, if, that is, attending weekly Mass is an integral part of being a member of the

---

1 Center for Applied Research in the Apostolate, "Frequently Requested Church Statistics," *Center for Applied Research in the Apostolate*, accessed December 20, 2016, http://cara.georgetown.edu/frequently-requested-church-statistics/.

Catholic Church. Based on the CARA survey, it seems that a significant number of self-identified U.S. Catholics do not think it is. Are they right? Who gets to decide if they are? Does the Church? And what if an individual person disagrees with the Church? What exactly does membership in the Catholic Church entail (see sidebar)?

Becoming a Member of the Catholic Church

Most people become members of the Church by being born into it; their parents are Catholic, so they become Catholic. For children who have reached the age of reason and for adults, there is a formal process to become a member called the Rite of Christian Initiation of Adults (RCIA). The process is separated into the following distinct periods and rites. For information on RCIA classes near you, call your diocese or local parish.

1. Precatechumenate:
A period of evangelization and learning about Jesus and his Church, discerning whether or not one is being called to be a member. If so, one celebrates the rite of acceptance.

2. Catechumenate:
A period of prayerfully considering the Scriptures, the teaching of the Church, and what it means to live as a baptized member. Participants are called catechumens, or those in whom the word of God echoes. The catechumenate can lead to the request for baptism.

3. Rite of election:
A person's request for baptism has been accepted, and he or she is now called "the elect." The elect enter into a period of purification during Lent, preparing to become a member of the Church.

4. Easter Vigil:
The elect receive the sacraments of initiation (baptism, confirmation, Eucharist) and participate in the Lord's Supper for the first time.

5. Mystagogy:
After being accepted into the Church, the newly baptized continue to pray and learn, understanding that they must persevere on the journey to heaven.

A good source for more information about the RCIA is the U.S. bishops website: www.usccb.org.

To answer these questions, one must consider the very specific things the Church has to say about membership within her ranks. But before looking at the specifics, it's important to address the underlying issue of Church authority. The Catholic Church proclaims that she was founded by Jesus Christ and that Jesus remains united to the Church as a head is united to its body. Before ascending into heaven, Jesus established a hierarchy among his followers, giving the keys of the kingdom to Peter, who led the early Church with the other apostles. They, in turn, handed on their authority to their successors, the pope and the bishops. All of them, from Peter on, exercised authority for the Church. The main task has always been to follow the path of Christ, to abide in him (see Jn 15:4). To support the union of head and members, the pope and bishops proclaim the Faith, preside over the sacraments and provide the service of leadership, which includes stipulating what constitutes membership in the Church.

What Makes a Member of the Church?

During Vatican II (1962-1965), Pope Paul VI, with the agreement of the assembled bishops, promulgated the Dogmatic Constitution *Lumen Gentium*, which sets forth the nature and mission of the Church. It also explains what entails membership in the Church. The requirements are expressed in a highly compressed manner: "They are fully incorporated in the society of the Church who, possessing the Spirit of Christ accept her entire system and all the means of salvation given to her, and are united with her as part of her visible bodily structure and through her with Christ, who rules her through the Supreme Pontiff and the bishops" (14).

This is a packed sentence, to say the least, and one needs to read it a few times in order to appreciate not only what it's saying but also what it's not saying. Certainly the requirements for membership are not surprising, for they include the basic elements that can be found in other ecclesial documents: union with Christ and other members through the Holy Spirit; acceptance of everything the Church is and teaches; remaining in relationship with the earthly institution and its leaders. These requirements are manifested outwardly by members through the "profession of faith, the sacraments and ecclesiastical government and communion" (*Lumen Gentium*, 14). In other words, a member of the Catholic Church believes what the creed teaches, participates in the sacraments, beginning with baptism, and gives proper obedience to Church leaders. However, notice that *Lumen Gentium* attributes all these necessities and dispositions to those who are "fully incorporated in the society of the Church," which begs the question: what about those not fully incorporated? Are they also members?

Membership and Canon Law

The normal way of becoming a member of the Church is through the sacraments of initiation: baptism, confirmation, and Eucharist. Children born to Catholic parents often receive these sacraments during the period between their birth and teenage years. Adults who want to join the Catholic Church do so mainly through the RCIA process. This excerpt from the Church's *Code of Canon Law* provides a more legal expression of membership:

Canon 204.1: The Christian faithful are those who, inasmuch as they have been incorporated in Christ through baptism, have been constituted as the people of God. For this reason, made sharers in their own way in Christ's priestly, prophetic, and royal function, they are called to exercise the mission which God has entrusted to the Church to fulfill in the world, in accord with the condition proper to each.

Canon 204.2: This Church, constituted and organized in this world as a society, subsists in the Catholic Church governed by the successor of Peter and the bishops in communion with him.

Canon 205: Those baptized are fully in the communion of the Catholic Church on this earth who are joined with Christ in its visible structure by the bonds of the profession of faith, the sacraments, and ecclesiastical governance.

Canon 206.1: Catechumens, that is, those who ask by explicit choice under the influence of the Holy Spirit to be incorporated into the Church, are joined to it in a special way. By this same desire, just as by the life of faith, hope, and charity which they lead, they are united with the Church which already cherishes them as its own.

Canon 206.2: The Church has a special care for catechumens; while it invites them to lead a life of the Gospel and introduces them to the celebration of sacred rites, it already grants them various prerogatives which are proper to Christians.

Canon 207.1: By divine institution, there are among the Christian faithful in the Church sacred ministers who in law are also called clerics; the other members of the Christian faithful are called lay persons.

Canon 207.2: There are members of the Christian faithful from both these groups who, through the profession of the evangelical counsels by means of vows or other sacred bonds recognized and sanctioned by the Church, are consecrated to God in their own special way and contribute to the salvific mission of the Church; although their state does not belong to the hierarchical structure of the Church, it nevertheless belongs to its life and holiness.

In fact, *Lumen Gentium* avoids describing in detail what constitutes membership apart from full incorporation. Other documents like the *Catechism of the Catholic Church* fill in the gap by offering a minimum standard for discernment purposes. *Lumen Gentium* takes for granted, of course, that there are people who are members of the Church and others who are not. For the latter group — other Christians, Jews, Muslims, and people who profess no faith (other Christians are a special case: although they are obviously not fully incorporated into the Catholic Church, they are members of the body of Christ by their baptism) — *Lumen Gentium* describes how they are related to the Church. But the intent of the document is not to provide a chart that lists various levels of membership with corresponding requirements. Rather, for those who are members, the clear intent is to exhort them to seek constantly the fullness of their baptism. In the Spirit of Christ, *Lumen Gentium* invites people to set their eyes on the goal of union with God, to reject complacency, and to persevere along the path that Jesus has provided, which includes the gift of the Church and all she has to offer.

However, *Lumen Gentium* does provide one very important caveat. In perhaps its boldest passage about membership, *Lumen Gentium* states that a member of the Church who satisfies all the requirements and maintains all the visible bonds, but who does so without the proper motive, suffers a fate worse than excommunication: "He is not saved, however, who, though part of the body of the Church, does not persevere in charity" (14). Being a member of the Church is not simply a matter of receiving a sacrament, having one's name in the parish register, and then waiting for Judgment Day — as if membership alone guarantees salvation. Love is the proper motive. Love, indeed, is the essential requirement for Church membership. Without love, a person may go through the motions of membership, but he or she is really disconnected from Christ and his members.

The Precepts of the Church

The precepts of the Church are set in the context of a moral life bound to and nourished by liturgical life. The obligatory character of these positive laws decreed by the pastoral authorities is meant to guarantee to the faithful the very necessary minimum in the spirit of prayer and moral effort, in the growth in love of God and neighbor:

• The first precept (**"You shall attend Mass on Sundays and holy days of obligation and rest from servile labor"**) requires the faithful to sanctify the day commemorating the Resurrection of the Lord, as well as the principal liturgical feasts honoring the mysteries of the Lord, the Blessed Virgin Mary and the saints; in the first place, by participating in the Eucharistic celebration, in which the Christian community is gathered, and by resting from those works and activities that could impede such a sanctification of these days.

• The second precept (**"You shall confess your sins at least once a year"**) ensures preparation for the Eucharist by the reception of the Sacrament of Reconciliation, which continues baptism's work of conversion and forgiveness.

• The third precept (**"You shall receive the Sacrament of the Eucharist at least during the Easter season"**) guarantees as a minimum the reception of the Lord's body and blood in connection with the paschal feasts, the origin and center of the Christian liturgy.

• The fourth precept (**"You shall observe the days of fasting and abstinence established by the Church"**) ensures the times of ascesis and penance which prepare us for the liturgical feasts and help us acquire mastery over our instincts and freedom of heart.

• The fifth precept (**"You shall help to provide for the needs of the

Church") means that the faithful are obliged to assist with the material needs of the Church, each according to his own ability. The faithful also have the duty of providing for the material needs of the Church, each according to his own abilities (CCC 2041–2043).

A Balancing Act

As a member of the Church, the balance is between living in this world and setting one's eyes on the next. To support this dual endeavor, the Church as a visible institution needs laws and precepts for the common good and edification of its membership. At the same time, the Church must guard against any attitude or policy that would suggest that simply maintaining the laws is sufficient for membership. By focusing on what it means to be fully incorporated in the society of the Church, *Lumen Gentium* aims to keep all members engaged and striving for the goal.

What answer, then, would a reading of *Lumen Gentium* give to the question at the beginning of this article based on the finding of CARA's survey: Are the self-identifying Catholics, who say that they do not attend weekly Mass, members of the Church?

One could answer that they are not members (much less fully incorporated), for a member would know that attending Mass on Sunday and all other holy days of obligation is a requirement. Not doing so is a grave sin (see CCC 2181), and to actually stop going altogether separates one from the Body of Christ. Moreover, the sin here is not simply refusing to follow a rule, but failing to honor one's relationship with God and neighbor (i.e., to persevere in charity). However, the survey does not state why these people do not attend Mass. It's possible that some of the respondents are homebound senior citizens or people living in an area without a resident priest. In both cases, there is no culpability because of their situations. To give an accurate answer about a specific person, one would need to inquire about other important details, like the person's knowledge and consent. The ultimate judgment, of course, belongs to God, as Jesus reminds us in the Gospel: "Let them grow together until harvest; then at harvest time I will say to the harvesters, 'First collect the weeds and tie them in bundles for burning; but gather the wheat into my barn'" (Mt 13:30).

The point here is not to dodge the question, but to emphasize (again) that membership in the Church is not a simple matter of satisfying requirements. Following rules and satisfying requirements play a part in membership, but love is central.

Balance: Christ as Our Model

The leaders of the Church have an important balance to maintain when it comes to laws. On the one hand, they need to avoid the error of regarding obedience to the law as more important than honoring one's relationship with God and neighbor. On the other hand, the opposite extreme must be shunned as well: being so lax in requirements that the idea of being a member of a body is lost. Their inspiration should always be Christ, who said man is not made for the law (see Mk 2:27), but also, "I have come not to abolish [the law] but to fulfill" (Mt 5:17).

Motive of Love

Regarding the specific requirement of attending Mass each Sunday, a member hopefully moves beyond having only a sense of obligation and begins to attend from the motive of love. Such a movement happens as one perseveres in prayer and love, and as one begins to glimpse the meaning of the Mass. Mass welcomes the assembled body of Christ, who, united to Jesus its head by the power of the Holy Spirit, offers thanksgiving to the Father. Mass is where each member of the body receives nourishment to continue the journey and to love their neighbor. Mass is an encounter among members who celebrate their fellowship, support each other, and receive Jesus' gift of himself in word and sacrament. Mass is the foretaste of full communion with God and one another, in which even the hosts of heaven participate. If a member of the Church perceives Mass for what it is, then the motive for attending will be less "I have to be there" and more "I want to be there."

Certainly, there are all kinds of requirements that are part of being a member of the Catholic Church. One need only consult the *Catechism*, the documents of Vatican II, and any number of papal documents. But if to look for a detailed list of requirements that ensure membership misses the mark completely. Being a member of the Church is about abiding in Christ, always seeking to yield more fully to God's love and to share his love with one's brothers and sisters.

— STUDY GUIDE PART 5 ————————————————

Belonging to the Church

STUDY

1. What makes one a member of the Catholic Church?

2. What is the one essential requirement for Church membership?

3. What is the difference between attending Mass out of love and attending out of obligation?

CONTEMPLATE

1. "The balance is between living in this world and setting one's eyes on the next." How do you live out this balance in your life? What do you need to do to maintain the balance?

2. If you know a self-identified Catholic who doesn't attend Mass, what might you be able to do to help them reconsider their decision?

3. What about the way you live your life would make someone want to become a Catholic?

APPLY

1. Becoming a member of the Catholic Church is a process. Consider some ways that you might help those who will be entering the Church this Easter.

2. The first precept of the Church is to attend Mass and rest from labor on Sundays and holy days. What is one way that you can "keep the Sabbath" this week?

3. According to the *Catechism of the Catholic Church*, baptism is "the first of the seven sacraments, and the 'door' which gives access to the other sacraments." Read and pray your baptismal promises, recommitting yourself to the Faith.

PRAYER

Act of Faith

O my God, I firmly believe
that you are one God in three divine Persons,
Father, Son, and Holy Spirit.
I believe that your divine Son became man
and died for our sins and that he will come
to judge the living and the dead.
I believe these and all the truths
which the Holy Catholic Church teaches
because you have revealed them
who are eternal truth and wisdom,
who can neither deceive nor be deceived.
In this faith I intend to live and die.
Amen.

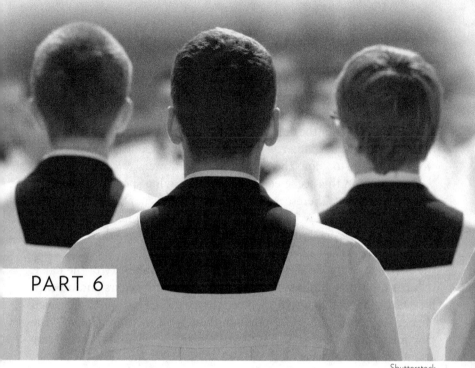

Answering God's Call

Walking home with her father, Louis Martin, after praying vespers with him on the feast of Pentecost on May 29, 1887, Saint Thérèse of Liseieux (1873–1897) fretted over telling him about the conviction she had reached through prayer regarding her vocation. The anxiety was not linked to the specific call, becoming a Carmelite nun; her worry was about timing, for she was only fourteen.

Louis worried too, and he told Thérèse that she was "still very young to make such a serious decision." Perhaps he wondered as well if Thérèse's resolve was influenced by the fact that two of her older sisters had already entered the Carmel at Lisieux: Pauline in 1882 and Marie in 1886. Thérèse, however, pleaded her cause so convincingly that she persuaded her father to give his consent.

After allowing Thérèse to pursue her vocation — she would, in fact, enter the Carmel almost a year later on April 9, 1888 — Louis gently took a little flower from the ground and told his daughter that God had brought it into being and sustained it ever since. Thérèse would never forget the image, nor the description of God's merciful action. She always maintained that her father was really speaking about her.[1] Hence, the world has come to know Thérèse as the "little flower."

Reflecting on this scene eight years later, having spent seven winters inside the convent, Thérèse recognized that she was not the only flower in God's garden. In what would eventually be published as her autobiography (*Story of a Soul*), she wrote: "All the flowers He has created are beautiful ... the splendor of the rose and the whiteness of the lily do not take away the perfume of the little violet or the delightful simplicity of the daisy. ... Just as the sun shines simultaneously on the tall cedars and on each little flower as though it were alone on the earth, so Our Lord is occupied particularly with each soul as though there were no other like it."[2] The task for each person, as Thérèse knew, is to accept humbly this divine attention and to be what God calls one to be.

Thérèse's image reflects beautifully the Church's teaching on vocations. Both Scripture and the *Catechism of the Catholic Church* reveal that God is intimately involved in bringing each person into existence.

From the Psalms:
"You formed my inmost being;
    you knit me in my mother's womb.
"I praise you, because I am wonderfully made;
    wonderful are your works!
My very self you know" (139:13–14).

From the *Catechism*: "The Word of God and his Breath are at the origin of the being and life of every creature" (703).

The care with which God creates each human being indicates the noble purpose he intends for them, and his intention is realized and fulfilled through the vocations he offers to men and women. Like flowers, vocations come in many varieties, but the Church distinguishes three basic kinds: a common call to every member of the human race; a

---

1 Thérèse Martin, *Story of a Soul: The Autobiography of St. Thérèse of Lisieux*, trans. John Clarke, 3rd ed. (Washington, DC: ICS Publications, 1996), 106–7.
2 Ibid., 14.

common call to every member of the Church; and, finally, the specific vocations that are addressed to individuals.

Called to Beatitude

The common call that God addresses to every member of the human race can be expressed as a goal or as an action. Either way, the end is the same: "God calls us to his own beatitude. This vocation is addressed to each individual personally" (CCC 1719). Beatitude, as defined by the Church, is not so much about happiness here and now, but, more fully, about eternal joy in God's presence (which certainly can be anticipated here and now).

The *Catechism* states: "God put us in the world to know, to love, and to serve him, and so to come to paradise. Beatitude makes us 'partakers of the divine nature' and of eternal life. With beatitude, man enters into the glory of Christ and into the joy of the Trinitarian life" (1721). Furthermore, "If, therefore, beatitude is the goal of each human person, then love is the way to get there. 'God who created man out of love also calls him to love — the fundamental and innate vocation of every human being'" (1604).

The objection might be raised that this common call is fine for those who believe in God, but it is not applicable to unbelievers. Certainly, the Church cannot force anyone to believe her teachings, but she can share with the world the truths she received via divine revelation. For example, it would not be far-fetched to maintain that each person desires to be happy. But where does this desire come from? The Church offers an answer: "The desire for God is written in the human heart, because man is created by God and for God; and God never ceases to draw man to himself. Only in God will he find the truth and happiness he never stops searching for" (CCC 27, see also 703).

Deep in the recesses of the human heart, there is a primordial memory of having been made by God and, as Saint Augustine said, "Our heart is restless until it rests in [God]" (cf. *Gaudium et Spes*, 19). Human beings at the dawn of creation chose to ignore this intimate connection with their Creator, but Jesus reminded the world of God's love by sacrificing himself on the cross and renewing the invitation to divine beatitude. The Church wants all people to know this good news.

The Call to Holiness

In fact, the second layer of vocation, which applies to every member of the Church, is focused precisely on making Jesus and his gift of salvation known: "The common vocation of all Christ's disciples, a vocation to holiness and to the mission of evangelizing the world" (CCC 1533). This includes Christians who are not members of the Catholic Church: "In this unity in mission, which is decided principally by Christ himself, all Christians must find what already unites them, even before their full communion is achieved. This is apostolic and missionary unity" (*Redemptor Hominis*, 12; see CCC 818, 1271, and *Lumen Gentium*, 15).

All who have received the gift of being baptized into Christ receive the corresponding blessings, but they also share in the same fundamental duty: to go out to all the world and proclaim the Gospel of Christ, so that others also may encounter him and know the hope of eternal life. It even can be stated more strongly: Jesus' disciples are called to live in such a way that other people encounter Christ through them, as Saint Paul said, "I live, no longer I, but Christ lives in me" (Gal 2:20).

This common call to the baptized to be holy and to spread the Gospel may seem like an impossible task. And it certainly would be if a person, or even the Church as a whole, were to attempt it apart from Christ. Baptism, however, unites the person to Jesus, and when one yields to this grace, the person shares in what the Church calls the three "munera" (i.e., the offices or missions) of Christ: priest, the sanctifying office; prophet, the evangelizing office; and king, the serving office. Indeed, the Church states that all the faithful participate in these munera "in accord with the condition proper to each" (*Code of Canon Law* 204.1).

What happens if a person is not aware of the good news of Jesus? If, as the Church teaches, it is part of human nature to love and to seek happiness, then a person without knowledge of Jesus may respond to these innate drives without knowing their source. God's grace is given independent of a person's recognition. If one lives according to the love of God implanted in one's heart, one can be saved. However, this lack of knowledge is not a good thing. The world has been given a gift beyond measure in Jesus. To say that it's possible to be saved without knowledge of him is not to suggest that ignorance of him should be accepted. It is far better to know Jesus than not to. Knowing him means knowing where one comes from and where one is headed. A person may have a sense that there is more to life than here and now, but without Jesus the person misses the full picture. Worse yet "some there are who, living and dying in this world without God, are exposed to final despair" (LG, 16). To work against this fate for anyone, the Church urges every member to share the Gospel.

Some may protest that such a call belongs to bishops and priests alone, those people who comprise the "official Church." However, this attitude is contrary to the Scriptures and the constant teaching of the Church. In the first place, there is only one Church, and, while there may be distinctions among members (and different roles), every member is part of the body. Clearly Saint Paul thought so: "now you are Christ's body, and individually parts of it" (1 Cor 12:27). And the Church in her documents echoes Saint Paul: "Therefore all the disciples of Christ, persevering in prayer and praising God, should present themselves as a living sacrifice, holy and pleasing to God. Everywhere on earth they must bear witness to Christ and give an answer to those who seek an account of that hope of eternal life which is in them" (LG, 10). In other words, no one is exempt from the call to holiness and sharing the gospel. If one is a member of the Church, then one shares the responsibility.

The Unique Call of Each Individual

That does not mean, however, that every member matures in holiness or preaches the gospel in the same way. Remember Saint Thérèse's image of the garden with many different, but equally beautiful, flowers. In just the same way, God gives particular gifts and talents to each person for the good of all, as Saint Peter reminds us: "As each one has received a gift, use it to serve one another as good stewards of God's varied grace" (1 Pt 4:10). Hence, a third layer of vocation as taught by the Church is the specific call God addresses to each individual.

In considering specific vocations, the Church distinguishes three different, but complementary, groups: the clergy, the laity, and those in consecrated life (CCC 873). "By divine institution, there are among the Christian faithful in the Church sacred ministers who in law are also called clerics; the other members of the Christian faithful are called lay persons [married and single people]. There are members of the Christian faithful from both these groups who, through the profession of the evangelical counsels [i.e., poverty, chastity, and obedience] by means of vows or other sacred bonds recognized and sanctioned by the Church, are consecrated to God in their own special way and contribute to the salvific mission of the Church; although their state does not belong to the hierarchical structure of the Church, it nevertheless belongs to its life and holiness" (CIC 207.1, 2).

Yet with such a diversity of vocations available in the Church, how can one come to a decision? Should one become a priest or a brother or a nun? What about marriage or the single life? And what about

Different Vocations

Clergy

Members of the clergy are divided into three orders: the episcopate (bishops), the presbyterate (priests), and the diaconate (deacons). Their primary focus is serving the other members of the Church by handing on the apostolic tradition. In terms of the three munera of Christ already mentioned, the clergy celebrate the sacraments (priestly office), preach the gospel at liturgies (prophetic office), and take care of the needs of the people, especially the poor and vulnerable (royal office, which includes governance of the Church, too).

Laity

The primary focus of the laity is to serve the world or the temporal order. They have a myriad of calls that are based on their individual gifts and talents. Lay people work in the fields of health care, education, government, skilled trades, and social services to name just a few. As baptized Christians, lay people become "the animating principle of human society" (CCC 899), bringing Christ into every encounter and workplace, and they use their gifts to contribute to the common good. Lay people also serve the world either as married or single persons. Married couples are to raise and form the children God gives them in the faith of Jesus and to help them anticipate heaven by loving their neighbor. Likewise, single people are called to embrace the opportunities they have to serve the one family of mankind. In their own practice of the three offices of Christ, the laity are priests insomuch as they offer their hardships and blessings as a sacrifice to God; they are prophets when they reflect Jesus to the world; and they are royalty when they take care of their neighbors' needs.

Consecrated Life

Those in consecrated life, as has already been mentioned, come from both the clergy and the laity. What distinguishes them is their voluntary acceptance of celibacy, poverty, and obedience. "It is the profession of these counsels, within a permanent state of life recognized by the Church, that characterizes the life consecrated to God" (CCC 915). Many of the men and women in consecrated life belong to religious orders like the Dominicans or Franciscans. Men can be brothers, monks, and priests. Women can be sisters and consecrated virgins and widows. Both men and women might be members of a secular institute. They also usually share in a particular apostolate such as working in schools or hospitals or homeless centers. Whatever their particular area of service might be, those in consecrated life have chosen to follow closely the life of Jesus, who also lived the counsels. Like Jesus, they want to remind everyone by their lives and service that, as good as this world is, it is not our final home.

becoming a doctor, a skilled craftsman, or a teacher? Actually, given the different personalities, life histories, and even the bio-medical make-up of people, the possibilities can be narrowed down quite a bit for any particular individual. Nevertheless, in coming to a decision, there are a few essentials: What does God want? What is one suited for? What does the community (i.e., family, friends, mentors, and the Church) think?

For most people, coming to a decision about a vocation will take a lot of time and prayer. There are, of course, exceptions: prodigies who have been blessed with an amazing talent, or people like Saint Thérèse, who reach a conviction quite young. The first step, however, is placing oneself in God's hands through prayer: "What is your will for me God? Speak, for your servant is listening." While it's unlikely that God will answer the prayer in an audible way, he does provide people with certain personalities and skill sets that can steer them in the right direction. A person who struggles in the physical sciences, but excels in literature and philosophy, may not be on a path toward becoming a doctor. Does one's personality augur for a life of celibacy or marriage? The point is that God speaks to people through the gifts he has given them, and those gifts should be developed and brought to bear in one's discernment. God also speaks to people through their loved ones, mentors, and the Church. A wise person listens very carefully to the opinions of those who know him or her well. Moreover, if one does discern a call to the clerical or religious life, then those who are charged with receiving candidates will test the call.

To put it succinctly, when one is discerning a vocation, one must pray, think, and act. Moreover, undergirding one's discernment must be a confident trust in the mercy and love of God. As Saint Thérèse discovered in her own discernment, the God who made each person with such great intimacy and care is not going to leave anyone in the dark.

There may be periods of frustration and impatience; it may even seem as if God is holding back. Often, however, setbacks and inconveniences are ways that God interrupts a person's logic in order to set him or her on the path he prefers. Indeed, many wise men and women who have spent their lives chasing passionately after God will testify that we need to be ready for surprises when making the effort to yield to him.

Nevertheless, the absolute, non-negotiable requirement to being what God calls us to be is to remind ourselves daily of God's love, even if it seems absent. For the Lord has spoken: "Can a mother forget her infant, be without tenderness for the child of her womb? Even should she forget, I will never forget you" (Is 49:15).

Answering God's Call

STUDY

1. What are the three basic kinds of vocations?

2. What are the three different but complementary groups of specific vocations?

3. What are the three "munera," or missions, of Christ?

CONTEMPLATE

1. With the diversity of vocations in the Church, how did you come to your decision about your own vocation? If you are still deciding, what are some factors to consider?

2. God has created each of us for a noble purpose. What is the difference between your purpose and your vocation?

3. Sometimes people think that those who comprise the "official Church" have more responsibility than others to spread the Gospel. Do you think that is true? Why or why not?

APPLY

1. Consider your vocation. How can you make a concerted effort to live your vocation more fully this week?

2. We are called to live in such a way that people encounter Christ through us. Choose one thing you can do tomorrow to show the world the face of Christ.

3. We each have special gifts given to us by God. Identify your special gift. Ask family and friends to help you discern if you are unsure.

PRAYER

Gracious God,

You have called me to life and gifted me in
many ways.

Through baptism you have sent me to continue
the mission of Jesus

by sharing my love with others.

Strengthen me to respond to your call each day.

Help me to become all you desire of me.

Inspire me to make a difference in others' lives.

Lead me to choose the way of life you have
planned for me.

Open the hearts of all to listen to your call.

Fill all with your Holy Spirit that we may
have listening hearts and

the courage to respond to you.

Amen.

— *United States Conference of Catholic Bishops*

PART 7

Shutterstock

Our Moral Compass

God, who is a communion of love (the Holy Trinity), created human beings to share in his love. As human beings, made by God in his image and likeness, we have an inherent dignity and the gifts of reason and freedom, which give us the capacity either to live in harmony with or to resist our Creator. Scripture and Tradition reveal that the first human beings misused their intellect and free will and chose to turn from God by sinning, disobeying the will of God that had been made known to them:

From Scripture:

"Then God asked: '... Have you eaten from the tree of which I had forbidden you to eat?'" (Gn 3:11).

From Tradition:

"From the very onset of his history man abused his liberty, at the urging of the Evil One. Man set himself against God and sought to attain his goal apart from God" (*Gaudium et Spes*, 13).

God, however, who is perfectly free, chose not to leave human beings in their sin. Instead, he chose to forgive them and to offer them a path toward reunion with him through Jesus Christ. "It is in Christ, Redeemer and Savior, that the divine image, disfigured in man by the first sin, has been restored to its original beauty and ennobled by the grace of God" (CCC 1701). Through his life, passion, death and resurrection, Jesus not only saves humanity but also shows them how to accept the offer of salvation: "I am the way and the truth and the life. No one comes to the Father except through me" (Jn 14:6). Therefore, if one wants to know the meaning and substance of Christian morality, then one needs to look at Christ.

The word "morality" is often defined as a set of principles that leads a person who adopts them to right conduct. A particular system of morality also tends to be linked with a teacher, like Aristotle or Immanuel Kant. As the term implies, "Christian morality" is linked to Christ, who, like any teacher, has rules and commandments that he shares with his disciples. More importantly, Jesus models for his disciples how to live. However, the aim of Jesus' instruction is not simply right living, or even happiness (although both are certainly included), but rather the fullness of life experienced in the communion of divine love. Union with God is the goal of human existence. Indeed, it is the original state of human beings (as has already been noted). Christian morality, therefore, is less an ethical system and more a school of love. Its master is Jesus Christ.

Love Is the Way

Jesus, of course, never used the term "Christian morality." Used here, the term refers to Jesus' teaching on love and the Church's principles that form a support for following the Lord's teaching. Sadly, many people have experienced great frustration in understanding Jesus' words. The rich young man in the Gospel, for example, wanted Jesus to state unequivocally that by obeying the commandments one would gain eternal life (Mk 10:17–31). When Jesus asked him to go deeper toward the spirit of the law, which calls for a complete gift of self to God and neighbor, the young man walked away.

Then there are those like some of the religious leaders at the time who hated Jesus precisely because he would set aside the letter of the law in order to heal someone (Mt 12:9–14) or to feed his hungry disciples on a Sabbath (Mt 12:1–8). Even those who seemed to recognize the centrality of love in Jesus' way of life wanted to know exactly how much love they had to give. Jesus answered with the parable of the Good Samaritan (Lk

10:29–37), which makes it clear that love does not simply satisfy the law, nor can it be measured. Love is the way and the goal; it moves toward wholeness and union, whether that means taking care of a neighbor or, ultimately, entering eternal life.

Love of God and love of neighbor: these two commandments are the substance and meaning of Christian morality. "There is no other commandment greater than these," Jesus says (Mk 12:31). Nevertheless, the force of Jesus' words, the fact that he is asking for wholehearted and completely selfless love, can be disconcerting, to say the least (see Mt 19:25). Who can even begin to live by these two commandments? It seems impossible. Yet Jesus does not say, "Try to love like me, or give it your best shot." He says, "As I have loved you, so you also should love one another" (Jn 13:34). Jesus takes it for granted that human beings can participate in his love by both receiving it and sharing it. They just need to be reminded.

Reason and Freedom

Fundamental to Jesus' good news is that he became man out of love for all men and women, to save us from our sins and eternal death. Moreover, Jesus lays down his life for us (Jn 10:15) in order to remind us of both our inherent dignity and our capacity to respond to his love. Created in the image and likeness of God, human beings have two gifts: reason, which enables them to understand "the order of things established by the Creator," and freedom, which enables them to direct themselves to their "true good," which is eternal life with God (CCC 1704). While we still suffer the consequences of original sin (and any personal sin), we need not remain enslaved to sin if we receive Jesus' forgiveness and mercy. Through the grace of forgiveness, we are able to follow Christ; we are capable of "acting rightly and doing good" (CCC 1709).

Yet knowing our inherent dignity and possessing the attributes (redeemed by Christ) to accept God's invitation to communion with him does not make it any easier to act on these good gifts. This is why the Church has sought to explain the way of Christ's love, or Christian morality, in a manner that is, perhaps, less daunting. While Jesus remains the author and archetype of Christian morality, and participating in divine love is its essence, the Church provides certain principles that can help a person respond better in receiving and sharing God's love.

Two fundamental principles that ground Christian morality are 1) "there is objective truth," and 2) "there is the 'good.'" Neither one is universally accepted as self-evident in the present culture. Nonetheless, the Church proclaims that God is the source of all truth and whatever is good. And human beings, through their reason and free will, are able to discern what is true and choose what it is good. Moreover, these qualities, inasmuch as they have their origin in God, do not change based on human culture. The dignity of the human person is an example of an eternal truth. The protection of innocent life is always a good to be achieved. In God's "economy," what is true and good for one person is true and good for another, and both are discernible through the use of reason and God's revelation.

Closely related to truth and goodness is what the Church calls

> "Freedom is the power, rooted in reason and will, to act or not to act, to do this or that, and so to perform deliberate actions on one's own responsibility. By free will one shapes one's own life. Human freedom is a force for growth and maturity in truth and goodness; it attains its perfection when directed toward God, our beatitude" (CCC 1731).

"natural law," which does not refer to nature in the sense of irrational beings. Rather, natural law "shows man [and woman] the way to follow so as to practice the good and attain [their] end," which is union with God (CCC 1955). The Ten Commandments express the principal precepts of the natural law. They teach us how to honor our relationship with God (the first three commandments) and with our neighbor (the last seven), which are ways of participating in the good. The Beatitudes proclaimed by Jesus in the Sermon on the Mount build upon the Ten Commandments by showing what a person who yields to the grace of God and imitates the life of Christ must do in love. Whereas the Ten Commandments are easily accessible to human reason, the Beatitudes (and the Sermon on the Mount in general) reveal "the countenance of Jesus Christ and portray his charity," in which his disciples are invited to share (CCC 1717).

Human beings, because we have free will and the offer of God's grace, are able to shape our lives according to the principles made known through natural law and revelation. We are able to choose between good and evil so long as we remain on earth. Freedom also makes us responsible for our acts: "It is the basis of praise or blame, merit or reproach" (CCC 1732). At the same time, the Church also teaches that the "imputability or responsibility for an action can be diminished or nullified by ignorance, duress, fear, and other psychological or social factors" (CCC 1746). Still, human acts — "that is, acts that are freely chosen in consequence of a judgment of conscience" — are either good or evil, and determining which depends on "the object chosen; the intention; and the circumstances of the action" (CCC 1750).

The object of an act is "a good toward which the will deliberately directs itself" (CCC 1751). What does the person want or desire? What is he or she looking for? Obviously, the ultimate good can and should be behind every subordinate good: "I want to get all A's in medical school so that I can better serve my brothers and sisters who are sick and give glory to God." "Getting A's" is an object, and it is a "good." But notice that the intention is crucial. If the person's intention had nothing to do with helping the sick, and was really only about guaranteeing a certain salary, then the act would lose its goodness. (Money, by the way, is not evil in itself, but the love of money is.) Finally, the circumstances "contribute to increasing or diminishing the goodness or evil of human acts" (CCC 1754). In the present example, a person who wants to do well in school out of fear of God is less good than the person who wants to give him glory.

"A morally good act requires the goodness of the object, of the end, and of the circumstances together. An evil end corrupts the action, even if the object is good in itself (such as praying and fasting 'in order to be seen by men'). The object of the choice can by itself vitiate an act in its entirety. There are some concrete acts — such as fornication — that it is always wrong to choose, because choosing them entails a disorder of the will, that is, a moral evil. It is therefore an error to judge the morality of human acts by considering only the intention that inspires them or the circumstances (environment, social pressure, duress or emergency, etc.) which supply their context. There are acts which, in and of themselves, independently of circumstances and intentions, are always gravely illicit by reason of their object; such as blasphemy and perjury, murder and adultery. One may not do evil so that good may result from it" (CCC 1755–56).

These principles that ground the practice of Christian morality may not be as daunting as Christ's commandment to love as he loves, but they certainly can seem rather complicated in the context of daily living. Does anyone really go through such a detailed analysis of their actions to make sure they conform to the Church's teaching on right conduct and Jesus' commandment of love? The answer is: hopefully not. For the most part, we engage these principles automatically after living the Christian faith for years, through a conscience that has been well-formed by prayer, study, and good habits. Still, the principles can be very helpful, even to mature Christians, in times of crisis or in matters that are difficult to discern. They can also provide support and grounding when responding to a culture that relativizes truth and goodness. Nevertheless, their real purpose is to free us to attain the good for ourselves and for our neighbor through a participation in divine love.

An analogy might be a better way to show how living by the principles of Christian morality blossoms into a participation in the love of Christ. Consider this: who is freer to play the piano? A person who has never played before, or the virtuoso who started playing when she was five years old and since then has dedicated countless hours to learning the notes, reading music, and perfecting the timing? Obviously, it is the virtuoso. Through her discipline and practice, and by developing her skill from the firm foundation of the fundamentals, the virtuoso now has the freedom to play the piano whenever she wants. Moreover, whereas the basic skills are still evident in her playing, she no longer thinks about them. Indeed, now that they have been formed into a good habit, they free her to express her own personality in the music.

The analogy, of course, is not perfect. Christian morality is not a discipline in the same sense as playing the piano, if for no other reason than Christian morality originates in the person of Jesus Christ, who is able to grant his gifts to whomever and however he pleases. Yet, the analogy is helpful. A person needs to know and understand the basic rules and commandments of Christ, and to put them into practice. The person, moreover, needs to be an active participant in a relationship with Jesus, reading and pondering his words, meditating on his deeds, and following his example. Receiving his grace and love, too, through participation in the sacraments, and then sharing these gifts with others, is part of anticipating the full communion in heaven. When desires conflict with this ultimate goal, the person must exercise the freedom to say "no" to self. All of these good practices build up a person both to receive and share the love of Christ.

As the author of the letter to the Hebrews wrote, "At the time, all discipline seems a cause not for joy but for pain, yet later it brings the peaceful fruit of righteousness (holy living) to those who are trained by it" (Heb 12:11). Indeed, when a person is immature in love, many of love's demands seem like an obligation. Yet, when love has matured, the demands are sweet and become an oblation to the One who is perfect Love. May each person, through the grace and love of Christ, enter this perfect Love who remains for all God the Father and the Son and the Holy Spirit.

— STUDY GUIDE PART 7 ————————————————

Our Moral Compass

STUDY

1. What is the aim of Jesus' instructions on morality?
2. What are the two fundamental principles that ground Christian morality?
3. What is the definition of freedom according to the *Catechism of the Catholic Church*?

CONTEMPLATE

1. "Jesus takes it for granted that human beings can participate in his love by both receiving it and sharing it." What does participating in Jesus' love mean to you?
2. Human beings are capable of choosing between good and evil. Why does it so often seem that evil is easier to choose than good?
3. "The ultimate good can and should be behind every subordinate good." What does that mean to you? How can this statement be a guide to moral decisions?

APPLY

1. We are all called to be active participants in a relationship with Jesus. What can you do today to improve your relationship with Jesus?
2. Christian morality is a school of love that helps us follow Jesus. How can you explain to someone that morality actually grants freedom, rather than restricts it?
3. We are told to love our neighbor as our self. This implies we are to love ourselves. What are some practical ways to love yourself that aren't selfish or self-centered?

PRAYER

My Lord God,
I have no idea where I am going.
I do not see the road ahead of me.
I cannot know for certain where it will end.
Nor do I really know myself,
and the fact that I think I am following your will
does not mean that I am actually doing so.
But I believe that the desire to please you
does in fact please you.
And I hope I have that desire in all that I am
    doing.
I hope that I will never do anything apart from
    that desire.
And I know that if I do this you will lead me by
    the right road,
though I may know nothing about it.
Therefore will I trust you always
though I may seem to be lost and in the shadow
    of death.
I will not fear, for you are ever with me,
and you will never leave me to face my perils
    alone.
— *Thomas Merton*

PART 8

The Catholic Conscience

Christian morality is a school of love that helps us grow in free-dom and follow Jesus, who is both the teacher and the wellspring of love. To help us live according to this school of love, each person has an inherent, God-given ability to judge, based on the principles of Christian morality, which personal acts help or hinder the attainment of eternal life with God. This is what is known as the conscience.

The conscience is aided in its task by the fundamental natural law: "Deep within his conscience man discovers a law which he has not laid upon himself but which he must obey. Its voice, ever calling him to love and to do what is good and to avoid evil, sounds in his heart at the right moment" (CCC 1776).

In essence, conscience is that "sacred place" in the human soul where "God speaks to man [and woman]" (*Veritatis Splendor*, 58). Made in the image and likeness of God, which means having the gifts of reason and free will, the human person is able to receive the natural law and apply it to concrete actions. The conscience will make "a judgment either of acquittal or of condemnation, according as human acts are in conformity or not with the law of God written on the heart" (VS, 59). Since the natural law directs the person to achieve the good in truth, the person who is listening to God's voice conforms his or her life, and every choice, to God who is "the first truth and highest good" (*Populorum Progressio*, 10).

> *"Freedom makes man a moral subject. When he acts deliberately, man is, so to speak, the father of his acts. Human acts, that is, acts that are freely chosen in consequence of a judgment of conscience, can be morally evaluated. They are either good or evil" (CCC 1749).*

Formation of Conscience

Needless to say, conforming our lives to God does not happen automatically. A child leaving the womb has to grow and mature not only in the use of reason and free will, but also in grace and love. The conscience also has to be informed and educated. On a very basic level, children will feel shame and even hide from their parents when they have done something wrong, but the same children will seek out their parents for praise when they have done something right. To help a child form his or her conscience well, parents and family, church and society, must continue their own formation by a "continuous conversion to what is true and to what is good" (VS, 64). At the same time, they must reject any negative influences such as sin or anything contrary to God's law and instead use the Ten Commandments and the Beatitudes to form good habits. A wonderful shorthand for forming a Christian conscience comes from Mary, who knows Jesus best, having witnessed his entire life: "Do whatever he tells you" (Jn 2:5).

When parents model for their children how to form the conscience, they also are demonstrating what it means to be in relationship with God. Even Jesus as a little boy learned from the good examples of Mary and Joseph how to honor God's law. Indeed, the formation of conscience is meant to happen within an intimate relationship with God. One of the greatest gifts a parent can give a child — or a mature Christian can pass on to a beginner in the Faith — is the example of a loving, faithful, and confident relationship with God (Father, Son, and Holy Spirit).

This relationship is marked by a spirit of obedience, but not in a mechanical or slavish sense. Rather, the mature Christian constantly renews the effort to adopt the attitude of Christ (see Phil 2:5–11), who always listened to the Father, fulfilled the Father's words, and trusted in the Father's love. Christians — trusting that God loves them and desires their salvation — learn and practice the Commandments and thereby build up the virtues, ready to bring about the good in every situation.

Such a life is not that of an automaton, blindly obedient, but of children who trust their parents, obeying in the root sense of the word, which denotes "attentive listening." It should be noted that there is nothing "childish" about this relationship. Its fruit, when lived well, fortifies the person in the courage and wisdom of Christ.

For most (if not all) of us, the formation of conscience is not a faultless path to eternal life with God. Especially in cultures that are indifferent or hostile to Christianity, there will be many obstacles. Hence the need for continual conversion to Christ, building upon the training from parents and mentors. In fact, mentors are not just for children. A Christian always can rely on the truth of divine revelation as expressed by the life of Christ and taught authoritatively by the Church when forming one's conscience. But it's a good practice to also have a regular confessor or spiritual director, a mature Christian adviser who is persevering in the Faith. Such a relationship moves beyond an acquaintance and involves correction and challenges as much as validation and approvals. One of the greatest dangers that every person needs to avoid in conscience formation is relying too much on personal feelings when making a moral judgment. Feelings can be powerful tools, and they should not be dismissed altogether, but a good spiritual director helps a person always to return to God's law as the moral gauge of one's actions.

> *"The truth about moral good, as that truth is declared in the law of reason, is practically and concretely recognized by the judgment of conscience, which leads one to take responsibility for the good or the evil one has done. If man does evil, the just judgment of his conscience remains within him as a witness to the universal truth of the good, as well as to the malice of his particular choice. But the verdict of conscience remains in him also as a pledge of hope and mercy: while bearing witness to the evil he has done, it also reminds him of his need, with the help of God's grace, to ask forgiveness, to do good and to cultivate virtue constantly."* — Veritatis Splendor, 61

Discerning God's Will

When one reaches the point of making a moral choice, one must appeal to one's conscience and "must always seriously seek what is right and good and discern the will of God expressed in divine law" (CCC 1787). If doubt exists or the conscience is uncertain, the judgment requires more prayer. When a certain judgment of conscience has been reached, it must be obeyed (see CCC 1790). A person who has made a judgment in conformity with the divine law will often have a deep sense of inner peace, even amid chaotic circumstances. A lack of peace, however, may signal that something is wrong; the person may need not only more discernment, but also more good counsel.

It is very important to note also that reaching a certain judgment in conscience does not necessarily mean that it is the right one, for a personal conscience can be in error about God's law. "Conscience is not an independent and exclusive capacity to decide what is good and what is evil" (VS, 60). That is the domain of God.

On the one hand, it's possible that negative influences, outside a person's responsibility, have warped the capacity to judge well. In this situation, a person has what the Church calls "invincible ignorance," and the person is not culpable for an evil committed, even though the action in question remains evil (and the person will still suffer the consequences of his or her choice). On the other hand, it's also possible that a person has willingly yielded to negative influences, or has failed to form his or her conscience, or has rationalized an evil choice in the hopes of achieving a future good (which is always wrong). In these cases the person would be culpable and would hopefully ask for God's forgiveness and mercy in order to remain on the path of conversion.

The subject of conscience is a foundational teaching of the Church, which is committed to handing on what it has received from Christ. One short article cannot offer a full treatment. In fact, no amount of reading or study alone will be able to provide a solid understanding of the reality of conscience. To be sure, one needs to read the Scriptures, the *Catechism*, and the magisterial teachings of the Church (like *Gaudium et Spes* and *Veritatis Splendor*). One also needs to accept, as the Church teaches, that there is an objective truth that can be known by every human being capable of rational thought. But the vital requirement for appreciating conscience remains entering and maturing in a deeply personal relationship with God, and this means listening to him and doing what he says after the appropriate discernment.

In order to see what a "working conscience" looks like in a relationship with God, consider the stories of Eve and Mary as told in Scripture. Both women are in a relationship with God and with a fellow human being. Both hear God's voice and receive a command (or a word) from him. And both make a choice that brings with it consequences. Although the word "conscience" never appears in either scriptural narrative, the conscience of each woman is active in her individual situation. Both demonstrate the teaching on conscience that the Church has passed on.

Eve and the First Temptation

In the book of Genesis, in the second story of creation (2:4 to 3:24), the inspired author uses the narrative to write about the relationship between God and the human person. We learn that God is the creator. He makes the world and everything in it, including man and woman. God provides them with everything they need to live in harmony with him and with each other. Genesis 2:9 states, "Out of the ground the Lord God made grow every tree that was delightful to look at and good for food." Moreover, he makes man and woman from the same "stuff," which underscores their equality and complementarity. The only commandment that God gives to the human beings is not to eat from "the tree of knowledge of good and evil."

In other words, they are to respect the relationship between God and themselves. He is the creator. He is the one who knows what is good and evil. Human beings are part of creation. They are a special part, enjoying the ability to think and to choose, which means they are made in God's image, but they remain creatures. It would be a sin to second guess or add to God's word. To ponder his word is fine; to understand it is better, a worthy goal; but to add to it or dismiss it is a sin. Our joy depends on listening to God and following him.

Yet, if we are made in the image and likeness of God, then we have the

"It is ... an error to judge the morality of human acts by considering only the intention that inspires them or the circumstances (environment, social pressure, duress or emergency, etc.) which supply their context. There are acts which, in and of themselves, independently of circumstances and intentions, are always gravely illicit by reason of their object; such as blasphemy and perjury, murder and adultery. One may not do evil so that good may result from it" (CCC 1756).

freedom to listen to God or not, to follow his words (or commandments) or not. Indeed, to remain in relationship with him or not. The tree of the knowledge of good and evil, from which God said the man and woman could not eat, becomes a source of temptation. If the other trees are delightful to look at and good for food, why not this one? The Evil One, personified in Genesis as the serpent, sees an opportunity here.

The serpent goes directly to the heart of the matter. He asks Eve, "Did God really say, 'You shall not eat from any of the trees in the garden?'" It seems like an innocent question; it's just a simple request for information. But the serpent's goal is to incite the woman to question God's commandment: What did God really say? The danger is real and terrible. If she even entertains the serpent's question, she already has listened to him instead of relying on God's word.

The woman, of course, does know what God said and, therefore, she should recognize the serpent's intentions.

Yet, she not only listens to the serpent but also offers an answer. And she does more than that. In an attempt to show just how much knowledge she has, she even adds to God's words: "You shall not eat it or even touch it, lest you die." But a quick review of Genesis reveals that God never said anything about touching or not touching the tree.

Eve has turned her thoughts away from God and is left to her own devices, which are not divine but "creaturely." The serpent is able to tell more lies, and Eve is an easy target. The serpent blatantly contradicts God and even suggests that God is a liar: "You certainly will not die!" So the woman, having abandoned God's commandment, relies only on her senses: She "saw that the tree was good for food and pleasing to the eyes, and the tree was desirable for gaining wisdom." And once again words — "gaining wisdom" — are added to God's word, this time by the serpent.

The woman makes a judgment based not on the commandment she received from God, but on the serpent's word and her senses. So she and Adam eat the fruit (he, by the way, is as guilty as she, because he also fails to listen to God).

The consequences of their sin are devastating. First, the relationship with God is so damaged that they want to hide from their creator. Second, their own relationship is damaged, as one can see when Adam puts all the blame on Eve. Third, they are banished from the garden and must now toil and labor in pain. And if all of that is not bad enough, they also pass on their sufferings to their progeny. Failing to listen to God is a sin and an evil that is destructive not only to the sinner but also to the whole family of mankind.

Mary: Righting Eve's Wrong

Mary's situation is in strong contrast to Eve's. The basic outline of Mary's life is well known. She is a simple woman, living in a little town, when God's word breaks upon her like the morning sun shattering the darkness of night. And God's word to Mary is specific: He tells her through an angel that she will conceive a baby in her womb through the power of the Holy Spirit (see Mt 1:18; Lk 1:31, 35).

Now Mary was a faithful Jew, so she would have been familiar with the Scriptures that describe irregular pregnancies (for example, Sarah giving birth in her old age to Isaac). Nevertheless, this word from God was unprecedented. When the angel announces the birth and says to Mary, "Hail, favored one! The Lord is with you" (Lk 1:28), Mary is troubled and ponders what the words mean. She even asks the angel, "How can this be, since I have no relations with a man?" (Lk 1:34).

The exchange is important because it shows that God's words (or commandments) are not always understood immediately and that a good amount of time dedicated to prayer may be needed before coming to any understanding or decision to act. Indeed, it is significant what Mary does not do: She does not pretend to understand something she in fact does not understand. Instead, by pondering God's word, she shows her willingness to continue to listen and to wait for God to make himself clear.

Notice, too, that Mary is not doubting that God can do what he says; she is making the effort to understand what he says. When the angel explains that the power of the Holy Spirit will make the conception possible, Mary gives her consent. (Joseph, by the way, who experiences his own crisis over Mary's situation, also gives his consent after listening to God.) Needless to say, Mary's decision bears fruit for everyone: the birth of Jesus and the gift of salvation.

Mary and Joseph honor their relationship with God and listen attentively to him, basing their judgments and actions on his words. They are unwilling to act hastily or to base their responses on their feelings and thoughts alone, even when God's word does not make much sense at first. They honor God's word by giving it appropriate discernment. Mary does not dismiss the angel's message as impossible, and Joseph does not divorce Mary as he intended, because through prayer God's word is clarified. Once God's word becomes clear to them, they act, trusting in God.

The human being, having been created by God, enters a relationship with God at the moment of conception. Gifted with reason and free will, the human person, using his or her conscience, is able to make a judgment between good and evil. The person is responsible for his or her acts and for forming the conscience. As the *Catechism* says, in this latter task, "[T]he Word of God is the light for our path; we must assimilate it in faith and prayer and put it into practice" (1785). The path enlightened by God's word is not always an easy one to travel, but it does guarantee freedom, peace of heart and the promise of heaven.

— STUDY GUIDE PART 8 ————————————

The Catholic Conscience

STUDY

1. How does *Veritatis Splendor* define "conscience"?
2. What are some ways that one forms a mature conscience?
3. What are the four consequences of the original sin of Adam and Eve?

CONTEMPLATE

1. Personal feelings play a role in making moral judgments. How can you decide when to trust your personal feelings and when to ignore them when making a decision?
2. One of the measurements of conformity with divine law is a sense of inner peace. What do you do when you are experiencing inner turmoil?
3. Sometimes you hear the argument that a lesser evil may be done so that a greater good will prevail. What is wrong with this argument?

APPLY

1. One of the greatest gifts we can pass on is the example of a loving relationship with God. What is one way you can show your family or coworkers your love of God today?
2. What are some ways that you can discern the will of God for you in a difficult situation?
3. "Conscience is that 'sacred place' in the human soul where 'God speaks to man [and woman]'" (*Veritatis Splendor*, 58). Use an examination of conscience as a guide to examining your own moral life.

PRAYER

Prayer of Contrition

O my God, I am heartily sorry for having offended thee, and I detest all my sins because of thy just punishments, but most of all because they offend thee, my God, who art all-good and deserving of all my love. I firmly resolve, with the help of thy grace, to sin no more and to avoid the near occasions of sin.

Called to Love

All of theology begins and ends in a simple but profound assertion: "God is love" (1 Jn 4:8). Based on this truth, the Catholic Church teaches that every human person is loved by God and called to love God and neighbor in return. The call is not exclusive to members of the Church, because God created each human being and gave each person the capacity to love. At the same time, it must be said that sin and evil have obscured the call and, therefore, the human response as well. Nevertheless, members of the Church, who are aware of the call through Baptism, and have freedom from sin and evil through Christ, have the responsibility to live by God's love and to share it with others (and thus it continues to be shared).

Saint Paul's hymn in his first letter to the Corinthians is a beautiful and faithful articulation of the Christian's fundamental stance in life:

If I speak in human and angelic tongues but do not have love, I am a resounding gong or a clashing cymbal. And if I have the gift of prophecy and comprehend all mysteries and all knowledge; if I have all faith so as to move mountains but do not have love, I am nothing. If I give away everything I own, and if I hand my body over so that I may boast but do not have love, I gain nothing. (1 Cor 13:1–3)

Paul may take credit for the artful arrangement, but the message is all Jesus. Jesus even makes it a commandment for his disciples: "love one another as I have loved you" (Jn 13:34). Nor did Jesus simply issue the command and walk away. Rather, in his concern that the disciples understand clearly what he meant, he demonstrated what love entails by his actions: " … he rose from supper and took off his outer garments. He took a towel and tied it around his waist. Then he poured water into a basin and began to wash the disciples' feet and dry them with the towel around his waist" (Jn 13:4–5).

However one interprets this scene of Jesus washing his disciples' feet, one can conclude confidently that Christ-like love manifests itself in humble service to one's neighbor, and that even power and authority are best applied through service. By "neighbor" Jesus means not only friends but also anyone in need, as he makes clear in his parable of the Good Samaritan (Lk 10:25–37).

The Parable of the Good Samaritan

The story of the good Samaritan in Luke's Gospel provides an excellent example of how we, as followers of Christ, should treat others:

To the question, "And who is my neighbor?" Jesus replied, "A man fell victim to robbers as he went down from Jerusalem to Jericho. They stripped and beat him and went off leaving him half-dead. A priest happened to be going down that road, but when he saw him, he passed by on the opposite side. Likewise a Levite came to the place, and when he saw him, he passed by on the opposite side. But a Samaritan traveler who came upon him was moved with compassion at the sight. He approached the victim,

> poured oil and wine over his wounds and bandaged them. Then he lifted him up on his own animal, took him to an inn and cared for him. The next day he took out two silver coins and gave them to the innkeeper with the instruction, 'Take care of him. If you spend more than what I have given you, I shall repay you on my way back.' Which of these three, in your opinion, was neighbor to the robbers' victim?" He answered, "The one who treated him with mercy." Jesus said to him, "Go and do likewise." (10:25–37)

God's call to love, while certainly applicable to our brothers and sisters in the faith, is also meant to move beyond Church boundaries. As the late Cardinal James Hickey was fond of saying: we love others "not because they're Catholic, but because we're Catholic."[1] The bottom line is that the service of love is integral to Christian discipleship, as Jesus says: "I have given you a model to follow, so that as I have done for you, you should also do" (Jn 13:15).

Quite a few people, in and out of the Church, have considered this commandment "to love as I have loved you" an impossible duty. But Jesus does not command the impossible. Whatever he asks his disciples to do, he provides the means to fulfill. Pope Benedict XVI, writing in his encyclical on love, *Deus Caritas Est* (DCE), explains Jesus' audacity by pointing to his generosity: "Love can be 'commanded' because it has first been given" (DCE, 14). Nowhere is this more vividly perceived than at Mass: "'Worship' itself, Eucharistic communion, includes the reality both of being loved and of loving others in turn. A Eucharist which does not pass over into the concrete practice of love is intrinsically fragmented" (DCE, 14).

Saint John puts it more simply: "We love because he first loved us" (1 Jn 4:19). If we want to avoid being "a resounding gong or a clashing cymbal," then every effort must be grounded in the love offered by Jesus.

This does not mean that we must make the effort to love God and others alone, or that it's even possible to do so, even if at times it feels like a lonely task. God, of course, remains the source of love. And while it is true that individual Christians must choose to yield to God's love and

---

1 Kristen Hannum, "Why social justice? 'Because we're Catholic,'" U.S. Catholic, July 2012, http://www.uscatholic.org/church/2012/06/why-social-justice-%E2%80%98because-we%E2%80%99re-catholic%E2%80%99 (accessed April 25, 2017).

incorporate its gifts into their lives, the practice of love is always carried out as a member of Christ's body. Perhaps it's best to say that loving includes both the individual and the communal effort. Pope Benedict XVI delineates the responsibility this way:

> Love of neighbor, grounded in the love of God, is first and foremost a responsibility for each individual member of the faithful, but it is also a responsibility for the entire ecclesial community at every level: from the local community to the particular Church and to the Church universal in its entirety. As a community, the Church must practise [sic] love. Love thus needs to be organized if it is to be an ordered service to the community. (DCE, 20)

On the personal level, each individual models himself or herself after Christ, whose love for all made him willing to die so others might live. It should be noted that the sacrifice of Christ is done from a position of strength in the sense of knowing his identity, being obedient to the Father's commands, and having confidence in the Father's fidelity. Jesus took on human nature in part to model for humanity how to be a faithful child of God, and the essential element in his life on this earth was the relationship with his Father. Jesus gained strength through this relationship, as he would tell his disciples: "I have food to eat of which you do not know" (Jn 4:32). Even in the midst of feeling like he had been abandoned, Jesus remained resolute in loving God and neighbor unto death because he was convinced that nothing could separate him from God.

The Christian, therefore, must realize his or her identity as an adopted child of God through Christ, fulfilling the words of God, and trusting in the gift of salvation. Being thus grounded is important, since practicing love as humble service to others can often feel like a great disadvantage. (And in a culture that does not value or even recognize God's love, perhaps it is — at least in passing matters.) However, the Christian keeps in mind the goal of eternal life through his or her relationship with God. Moreover, frequent prayer, reception of the sacraments, and life in a Christian community help the individual Christian to persevere in fulfilling the service of love. As one perseveres, one begins to perceive how love is its own reward, and that it engenders a deep sense of peace and confidence in God. In other words, the eternal advantages of loving well far exceed the temporary advantages of a "me-first" modus operandi.

But what does a life of love look like for the individual member of the Church here and now? Jesus answered similar questions by stating that it all boils down to two main commandments: love of God and love of neighbor (Mt 22:34–40). The Ten Commandments and the Beatitudes expand on Jesus' answer, and so do many of his parables, like the Good Samaritan (already mentioned) and the judgment of the sheep and goats (Mt 25:31–46). What we learn from Jesus is that his disciples are to feed the hungry, clothe the naked, visit the imprisoned. Disciples do not cheat or steal or gossip or kill. They honor their relationships, incorporating and subordinating each relationship within the relationship with God. In other words, the Christian disciple anticipates the life of heaven through life on earth.

There is no rule book that can cover every imaginable situation with which a person may be confronted, which is why the relationship with God and relying on his good graces is so important. As we yield more and more to God, putting on the mind of Christ, we are conformed to the way of Christ's love. We should not have to spend too much time wondering about what love requires in most daily decisions. For more difficult and complicated situations, we need to pray and think and act. What does Jesus say? What would he do? What is best for the person or persons involved? What action will best respect their ultimate destiny? More serious matters deserve more serious prayer and thought.

The Church, in her role of handing on the Faith, can be helpful in discerning the loving thing to do in a specific situation. The Church has developed principles based on Jesus' words that assist each member in loving well, and they constitute what has come to be called the social teaching of the Church. The first principle that guides every decision to love is the inherent and inalienable dignity of each human being. Love will not act contrary to the dignity of the human person, but will seek the good for that person (always keeping in mind the ultimate good of union with God in heaven). Therefore, innocent people (including children within the womb) cannot be murdered, persons cannot be used as things, and every person deserves the basic necessities of life, including work, nutrition, shelter, employment, and medical care. Moreover, loving after the model of Christ means being attentive to those who are neediest and most vulnerable and cast off from society.

Pope Francis said in an April 2017 TED talk — a first for a pope — that "we all need each other."[2] The "future is, most of all, in the hands of those people who recognize the other as a 'you' and themselves as part of an 'us.'"[3] So, in addition to the foundational principle of Catholic social teaching, there are three others that highlight the "us" of society. Christians are called to work for the common good, even at times freely foregoing a private privilege for the benefit of the community. Traffic laws are a simple example because they inhibit an individual's freedom of movement so that a greater number of individuals may travel safely. The second principle is subsidiarity, by which the Church means that "a community of a higher order should not interfere in the internal life of a community of a lower order" (CCC 1883). For example, the government should refrain from regulating the private activities and concerns of the family. The third principle is solidarity, which echoes the sentiment expressed by Pope Francis in the TED talk, that the human community

Catholic Social Teaching

The permanent principles of the Church's social doctrine constitute the very heart of Catholic social teaching. These are the principles of: the dignity of the human person, which has already been dealt with in the preceding chapter, and which is the foundation of all the other principles and content of the Church's social doctrine; the common good; subsidiarity; and solidarity. These principles, the expression of the whole truth about man known by reason and faith, are born of "the encounter of the Gospel message and of its demands summarized in the supreme commandment of love of God and neighbor in justice with the problems emanating from the life of society." In the course of history and with the light of the Spirit, the Church has wisely reflected within her own tradition of faith and has been able to provide an ever more accurate foundation and shape to these principles, progressively explaining them in the attempt to respond coherently to the demands of the times and to the continuous developments of social life. (Pontifical Council for Justice and Peace, Compendium of the Social Doctrine of the Church, English ed. [London: Bloomsbury Publishing, 2005].)

---

2 Pope Francis, "Why the only future worth building includes everyone," trans. Elena Montrasio, TED Conferences, LLC, April 26, 2017, https://www.ted.com/talks/pope_francis_why_the_only_future_worth_building_includes_everyone?language=en (accessed October 18, 2017).
3 Ibid.

enjoys not only a common beginning but also shares a common responsibility toward one another.

These principles are lived out in a personal way through acts of charity and the practice of the corporal and spiritual works of mercy (individuals helping others in need, family members taking care of each other, etc.). However, it does not take long to realize that individual efforts alone cannot make a dent in terms of responding to many of society's ills. This in no way denigrates one human being helping another; giving some money or providing a meal to a homeless person may be the one act of charity he or she receives that day. Who knows what that kind act might spark? But there remains the larger problem of homelessness (not to mention other problems), which requires what Benedict XVI calls the Church's practice of love: all the members together providing "an ordered service to the community."

And love has been organized from the very beginnings of the Church. As soon as Jesus ascended into heaven, Christian communities began serving all people, fellow believers and strangers alike. Saint Paul, who received the love of Jesus in a powerful way on the road to Damascus, traveled throughout the Mediterranean basin going from church to church, gathering a collection of money for the poor in Jerusalem (See 1 Cor 16:1–4; 2 Cor 8:1—9:15; Rom 15:14–32). In the post-apostolic age, "pagans were struck by the Christians' concern for the needy of every sort," and thereby testify to the Church's outreach (DCE, 22). By the mid-fourth century, institutions within monasteries and dioceses called "diaconiae" were established "for the service of charity" (DCE, 23).

Service in the Early Church

The "diaconia" was an institution of the early Church within monasteries and dioceses that carried out "an essential responsibility of the Church, namely a well-ordered love of neighbor" by providing social services (DCE, 21). In fact, the diaconia served its community so well that local governments took notice and sought out a partnership. In Egypt by the sixth century, the diaconia "had evolved into a corporation with full juridical standing, which the civil authorities themselves entrusted with part of the grain for public distribution" (DCE, 23). In Naples during the same time period, Pope Gregory the Great "was aware of a diaconia system that resembles what can often be found in state welfare programs today:

Governments distribute block grants to local organizations that are trusted to use those funds to care for the poor." (Brian J. Matz, "Early Christian Philanthropy as a 'Marketplace' and the Moral Responsibility of Market Participants," in *Distant Markets, Distant Harms: Economic Complicity and Christian Ethics*, ed. Daniel K. Finn [Oxford: Oxford UP, 2014], 120.)

These institutions of the local churches would distribute food and clothing, and provide housing and medical assistance to anyone in need.

The diaconia system is far removed from the twenty-first century in terms of time, and other church organizations have taken its place (like the Caritas Internationalis and Catholic Charities ministries), but the call it responded to and the services it provided are the same for every era. The Church in her ordered service to the community still heeds Jesus' command to "love one another as I have loved you." And whether it's distributing grain to a community five hundred years ago or providing shelter to a homeless person today, the particular service remains grounded in the same principles: the inherent dignity of each human person and the attainment of the common good through subsidiarity and solidarity.

When all is said and done, God's call to love, both as an individual and as a member of the Church, is about honoring the relationships we have: with God and with others. Our love for God is manifested in love for our neighbor: "If anyone says, 'I love God,' but hates his brother, he is a liar; for whoever does not love a brother whom he has seen cannot love God whom he has not seen" (1 Jn 4:20). Those who have accepted God's love take care of themselves and their families as a service of love. This is an application of subsidiarity based in the principle of human dignity. However, our service does not end with our individual family. As time and resources allow, we are called to serve our brothers and sisters by sharing time, talent, or treasure. This is an application of solidarity. Both kinds of service uphold human dignity and the common good. They also honor God by returning the love he gives, yielding a most fruitful harvest.

— STUDY GUIDE PART 9 —————————————————

Called to Love

STUDY

1. Who does Jesus mean when he tells us to love our neighbor?

2. What are the three principles of the Church's teaching on social doctrine?

3. What must all Christians do if they are to honor the call to love that comes from God?

CONTEMPLATE

1. All of theology begins and ends with the statement "God is love." What does that mean to you? How do you experience God's love in your life?

2. God's call to love is meant to move beyond Church boundaries, even to our enemies. How can you love someone like a terrorist or a mass murderer?

3. "The practice of love is always carried out [by a Christian] as a member of Christ's body." How does this apply to love of your family? To your personal relationship with God?

APPLY

1. One of the greatest gifts we can pass on is the example of a loving relationship with God. What is one way you can show your family or coworkers your love of God today?

2. "Christians are called to work for the common good, at times even freely foregoing a private privilege for the benefit of the community." What is a private privilege you enjoy in your family or at work that you could give up for the common good?

3. Choose one of the corporal or spiritual works of mercy to put into practice this week.

PRAYER

O my God! I offer Thee all my actions of this day for the intentions and for the glory of the Sacred Heart of Jesus. I desire to sanctify every beat of my heart, my every thought, my simplest works, by uniting them to Its infinite merits; and I wish to make reparation for my sins by casting them into the furnace of Its Merciful Love.

O my God! I ask thee for myself and for those whom I hold dear, the grace to fulfill perfectly Thy Holy Will, to accept for love of Thee the joys and sorrows of this passing life, so that we may one day be united together in Heaven for all Eternity. Amen

— *Saint Thérèse of Lisieux*

PART 10

Shutterstock.com

Prayer

Many people might struggle to define prayer these days, but whether one is religious or not, we tend to recognize its many forms: the woman kneeling in deep contemplation before the Blessed Sacrament; a family thanking God before sharing dinner together; the choir member joyfully belting out a song of praise; or the man muttering desperately about a financial predicament while driving to work.

We see a variety of approaches and methods when it comes to prayer, even different body postures. But this shouldn't lead us to believe that prayer is a method — something people do — when the reality is much deeper.

The *Catechism of the Catholic Church* defines prayer, first and foremost, not as a method, and not simply as an act of the human being, but as a "vital and personal relationship with the living and true God" (2558).

Why the distinction? If we start with methods and personal acts, then we might get the idea that the human being initiates prayer. Yet prayer is, essentially, a relationship with God, and God as the creator and source of

99

life is the one who begins prayer.

The relationship with God is similar to (but not the same as) the relationship with one's parents. When we are newborns, we do not enjoy a vital, personal relationship with our parents. They provide all of our needs and take care of everything. We do relate to our parents, in the sense that we "know" we need them. As babies, we cry out for our moms and dads when we are alone or afraid or needy. But the relationship is very basic. It's only when we grow and come to understand what our parents have done, what they have sacrificed, that we can appreciate their love and enter a reciprocal relationship with them.

Similarly, the relationship with

"Man may forget his Creator or hide far from his face; he may run after idols or accuse the deity of having abandoned him; yet the living and true God tirelessly calls each person to that mysterious encounter known as prayer. In prayer, the faithful God's initiative of love always comes first; our own first step is always a response. As God gradually reveals himself and reveals man to himself, prayer appears as a reciprocal call, a covenant drama" (CCC 2567).

God may begin with a vague sense about a power out there. We know that we did not make ourselves, and something must have happened to get the world started. So, in time, we begin asking some very basic questions: Who am I? Why am I here? Where did I come from? Where am I going? What is the meaning of life? It's when we start to ask these questions (or ones like them) and search for answers that the relationship with God begins for us on a conscious level.

Often the questions about the mystery of life are prompted by feelings of restlessness or a sense that we are missing something, and these feelings can coincide with a desire to be whole. Feelings of incompleteness also may overlap with a sense of wonder about the beauty of creation and how we fit into the world. What we are experiencing with these sentiments is the call from God beckoning us to become aware of his love, the same love that sustains us from the first moment of our existence in our mother's womb.

God's call comes to us in various ways which aid us in listening to him. "He made from one the whole human race to dwell on the entire surface of the earth, and he fixed the ordered seasons and the boundaries of their regions, so that people might seek God, even perhaps grope for him and find him, though indeed he is not far from any one of us. For 'In him we live and move and have our being'" (Acts 17:26–28).

Creation, in and of itself, (including our own existence) proclaims the grandeur and glory of God. Salvation — and most vividly the relationship of God with the Jewish people — reveals his fidelity and care for his people. Indeed, all of our relationships can be vehicles for coming to realize God's presence in our lives. But the greatest revelation of God and his love for humanity is not an act, but a person: Jesus Christ. Jesus reveals God to us in the flesh. For Christians, Jesus is where we begin to deepen our relationship with God. Jesus is the means for us to build and enjoy a vital and personal relationship with God — in other words, to enter into prayer.

> Some people have difficulty relating to God as a father. It may be that their relationship with their dads was not good or they have had bad experiences with men in general. Certainly their feelings should be respected. At the same time, it's worth noting that God is not a "father" in the way that human males are fathers. God is not male or female. He is spirit. What we can say is that God is the perfection of both motherhood and fatherhood. Parents are called to imitate the attributes of God and represent faithfully the divine relationship of God to his children. Jesus called God "father" and made known the good attributes of that title, which include (among others) love, mercy, kindness, generosity, forgiveness, and justice.

Jesus: Model of Prayer

When the disciples first encountered Jesus, they were attracted by his teaching authority and his powerful miracles. Moreover, we read in the gospels that many of the crowds that gathered around Jesus were interested in his ability to perform signs — and that's where the acquaintance ended for many of them (cf. Jn 6:1–15). The disciples, however, desired a deeper relationship with him and with God, whom Jesus referred to as his Father. So, with real desire, they asked Jesus, "Lord, teach us to pray" (Lk 11:1).

Jesus answered with the "Our Father" (See Mt 6:5–15; Lk 11:2–4), which is the basis for all the praying that we do since it is an acknowledgement of the relationship that exists between us and God. And the "Our Father" contains all the elements of prayer that we need in order to deepen the relationship.

We begin by naming God as our Father and our Creator. We acknowledge him for who he is. We bless his holy name; we praise him. We petition him that his will, not ours, be done in our lives and that his kingdom, not ours, comes into its fullness. We also acknowledge him as the one who provides for us and sustains us in life. At the same time, we trust that he will provide by asking him to give us our daily sustenance. He is also the Father of our eternal life, so we ask for forgiveness of our sins and the strength to persevere through trials, and ultimately death. In short, it is a prayer of confidence in God as the one who loves us and will bring us home to him.

Another very important aspect to the "Our Father" is made clear by the first word: "our." It's only three letters, but it is essential to understanding what our relationship with God entails. We do not say "My Father," but "Our Father." In other words, even if we pray alone, we always approach God conscious of the truth that our relationship with him places us in relationship with each other. So neither do we ask for "my daily bread" or "forgive my sins," but "our daily bread" and "forgive us our sins." We do not expect to receive these gifts if we are not willing to share them with others. If God is good to us, then we are called to be good to each other.

> The "Our Father" is handed on to us by both Matthew (6:9–13) and Luke (11:2–4). Matthew gives seven petitions, and Luke gives five. Why the difference? It's hard to know exactly, but it certainly might be the case that Jesus taught the prayer numerous times to different groups of people at different locations, so perhaps Matthew and Luke heard different versions. Nevertheless, the same basic points are made in each version.

Jesus, of course, provided much more than words when teaching his disciples how to pray; he also provided an example. As the *Catechism* states, Jesus is "the master and model of our prayer" (2775). So, if we had any doubt that prayer is, essentially, a relationship with God, then all we have to do is read the gospels. Everything that Jesus did — all of his teaching and preaching and healing — was done within the context of his relationship with the Father (which always includes the Holy Spirit). Jesus clearly loved all the people with whom he met, and he continues to love all of us still. Yet, this love for people is always subordinated to his love for the Father. Indeed, Jesus teaches us that if we want to love our neighbor well, we must love God first, or, to put it another way, our love for others flows through our love for God. Nowhere is this portrayed more dramatically than when Peter tries to persuade Jesus to forgo the cross. Jesus' response is immediate and firm: "Get behind me, Satan! You are an obstacle to me. You are thinking not as God does, but as human beings do" (Mt 16:23). Needless to say, by honoring the relationship with God, Jesus not only honors his relationship with us, but also wins our salvation.

In his relationship with the Father, Jesus also practices prayer in a number of ways. He often makes time to be alone with God, going off to a quiet place, where he can speak with the Father heart to heart, so to speak (Lk 5:16). We also see Jesus, in the gospels, taking part in communal liturgies of the day (Jn 2:12–14; Lk 2:41–42), and in some cases even reading and interpreting the Hebrew Scriptures (Lk 4:16–21). Jesus knew the Scriptures well, and quoted them often (even on the cross; Lk 22:37; Mt 27:46), so we can take for granted that reading the Scriptures was a regular part of his prayer life.

And although we could certainly fill many books on the subject of Jesus' prayer, we should also take notice of his perseverance. In addition to praying often, Jesus continued to pray even when it was difficult. The dark moment in Gethsemane, just before he began his journey to Golgotha, is the best example: despite the understandable feeling of wishing that his suffering could be bypassed, Jesus placed the situation in prayer (Lk 22:39–46). The model of prayer that Jesus provides for us is multifaceted, but it is grounded in a confident and trusting relationship with God and manifested by his love for the world.

> "The only way to pray is to pray; and the way to pray well is to pray much. If one has no time for this, then one must at least pray regularly. But the less one prays the worse it goes."
>
> — Abbot Chapman, quoted in Michael Casey, Sacred Reading: The Art of Lectio Divina (Liguori, MO: Triumph Books, 1995), 22.

Obviously we would do well to follow "our master and model" of prayer. And we can start by acknowledging that our relationship, which was started by God, is sustained by the Holy Spirit and Jesus. We will not reach the fullness of our relationship with God here on earth, but it is good to know that the good efforts we make here, even if they are clumsy, are not empty. As Saint Paul reminds us, "the Spirit too comes to the aid of our weakness; for we do not know how to pray as we ought, but the Spirit itself intercedes with inexpressible groanings" (Rom 8:26).

The Church Teaches Us about Prayer

Jesus also continues to provide for us today through his body, the Church, which, inasmuch as she is united to her head, helps us to follow his example. Over the two millennia that the Church (or the people of God) has practiced and pondered the gift of prayer, she has developed a rich tradition that includes different forms and expressions of communicating with God. The *Catechism*, which is separated into four main parts, devotes the last part entirely to prayer. This positioning is not an accident; it's meant to emphasize that all the preceding knowledge contained in the first three parts means little if it is not integrated into a loving relationship with God and neighbor.

Reading Part Four of the *Catechism* is well worth the time and effort. Although it includes definitions of prayer and examples, it is by no means a simple catalogue or index, but a real appreciation and articulation of the reality of prayer. The *Catechism* begins its meditation by looking at the relationship of the Jewish people with God and how that relationship was lived and fulfilled by Jesus (it also offers an exegesis of the Lord's Prayer). The *Catechism* demonstrates how the Church followed Jesus' example, including forms of prayer practiced by the early Church and still practiced today. It also offers advice on maintaining a prayer life by presenting witnesses to prayer like the saints and expressions of prayer like meditation and contemplation.

In keeping with the essential nature of prayer as a relationship with God, the *Catechism* points to the Eucharist as containing and expressing all forms of prayer: "it is 'the pure offering' of the whole Body of Christ to the glory of God's name" (2643).

The *Catechism* thus brings us back to the source and fulfillment of our prayer: God himself. We begin in him and end in him. Yet we still might have questions about prayer in the meantime: How do I know if I am praying well? If I am doing it right?

The number one principle is this: begin! We have to remember that God is a partner in this relationship (indeed, he is the greater partner). He is not going to give us a nickel if we need a dime! Certainly, it can be difficult to have confidence and trust in God, especially if our other relationships have suffered infidelity and pain. But that is why Jesus modeled for us how a human being is to relate with God. Like Jesus did, we have to make time for prayer (and not just a quick dash in and out).

We need time for individual prayer and for communal prayer. In the time we spend alone, we can read and ponder the Scriptures as Jesus did; we can tell God our needs and fears; we can ask him to help others; and we can praise and thank him. When we pray with others, we can do so actively and attentively, especially at the Sunday Eucharist, which we should not miss except for a grave reason so as not to weaken our relationship with God and the Body of Christ. If we are tempted to skip Mass, we might bring to mind our brothers and sisters who need our presence, just as we need theirs, as a help in faithfulness. Finally, we can follow the example of Christ by persevering in prayer, even when it is difficult and it seems that no one is listening, because the truth is this: Someone is.

STUDY GUIDE PART 10

Prayer

STUDY

1. How does the *Catechism of the Catholic Church* define prayer?
2. What are the five forms of prayer in the *Catechism*?
3. What are some of the ways that Jesus practiced prayer?

CONTEMPLATE

1. "Jesus continued to pray even when it was difficult." Persisting in prayer when there does not seem to be answer is challenging. What are some ways that you use to keep praying when prayer seems almost impossible?
2. "Prayer is, essentially, a relationship with God ... who begins prayer." What does it mean to you that God begins prayer? Is prayer always a response to God?
3. The saints have said that silence can be a great prayer. What is your experience with silence as prayer? Is it easy or hard?

APPLY

1. Go through the Our Father phrase by phrase. What does each phrase mean to you?
2. The *Catechism* says that the expressions of prayer are vocal, meditation, and contemplation. Which form of prayer do you use the most often? Consider incorporating another expression into your prayer life.
3. Saint Thérèse of Lisieux says that prayer is a "cry of gratitude." This week take time to write down at least one thing each day that you are grateful for.

PRAYER

I will extol you, my God and king;
  I will bless your name forever and ever.
Every day I will bless you;
  I will praise your name forever and ever.
Great is the LORD and worthy of much praise,
  whose grandeur is beyond understanding.
One generation praises your deeds to the next
  and proclaims your mighty works.
They speak of the splendor of your majestic glory,
  tell of your wonderful deeds.
They speak of the power of your awesome acts
  and recount your great deeds.
They celebrate your abounding goodness
  and joyfully sing of your justice.

— *Psalms 145:1–7*

PART 11

The Communion of Saints

Catholics believe that life continues after death and that a real communion exists among those who have not rejected Jesus. This bond is not destroyed by death because Jesus conquered death's power through his resurrection.

Life after death has always been a hope for human beings, a great many of whom throughout the centuries have recoiled at the thought of nothingness beyond the grave. A desire for the afterlife is reflected in ancient literature like Homer's *Odyssey* (in which Odysseus travels to the underworld) and even in the building of the Egyptian pyramids, which were thought to be landmarks that helped the soul travel to and from the hereafter. With Jesus, the hope of eternal life is realized, as he says to his disciples before his passion and resurrection:

Do not let your hearts be troubled. You have faith in God; have faith also in me. In my Father's house there are many dwelling places. If there were not, would I have told you that I am going to prepare a place for you? And if I go and prepare a place for you, I will come back again and take you to myself, so that where I am you also may be (Jn 14:1–3).

Saint Paul, writing to the Corinthians after Jesus' ascension into heaven, defends the teaching against naysayers: "If there is no resurrection of the dead, then neither has Christ been raised. And if Christ has not been raised, then empty too is our preaching; empty, too, your faith. ... But now Christ has been raised from the dead, the firstfruits of those who have fallen asleep" (1 Cor 15:13–14, 20).

Jesus is the life of the world, and anyone who remains in him — before or after death — continues to share in his life: "All things came to be through him, and without him nothing came to be. What came to be through him was life, and this life was the light of the human race; the light shines in the darkness, and the darkness has not overcome it" (Jn 1:3–4). Indeed, nothing can separate a person from Christ except one's free decision to reject him (Rom 8:35–39).

Saint Paul uses the image of a human body to describe the bond between Jesus and his followers: "As a body is one though it has many parts, and all the parts of the body, though many, are one body, so also Christ" (1 Cor 12:12). The words of Saint Paul, which describe the spiritual reality of living in Christ, prepared the way for the Church to articulate its teaching on the Communion of Saints.

Holy Things

When one reads or hears the phrase "the Communion of Saints," it may be that one thinks only of those people whom the Church remembers on All Saints Day. Certainly these are included, but the word "saint" is not exclusive to those declared so by the Church, as will be made clear later in this article. "The Communion of Saints" is a much broader and multivalent reality that, as the *Catechism of the Catholic Church* points out, can be organized under two main headings: "*sancta*," or communion in holy things; and "*sancti*," communion among holy persons (see 948)

As to which comes first, there is no chicken or egg problem to solve, for the "holy things" are what build up and unite the "holy persons." The Church "exists because of a common sharing in the goods [or *sancta*] of salvation, especially in the Eucharist."[1]

These goods are made available to the members of the Church through Christ, who remains the head of all the faithful who form his body (CCC 947). Saint Thérèse of Lisieux had a deep appreciation for the "*sancta*." In her characteristically bold manner, she seized upon this teaching and prayed to God, saying: "Since You loved me so much as to give me Your only Son as my Savior and my Spouse, the infinite treasures of His merits are mine. I offer them to You with gladness ... I offer You, too, all the merits of the saints (in heaven and on earth), their acts of *Love*, and those of the holy angels."[2]

Thérèse understood that she could receive the *sancta* and then offer them back to God for the salvation of all her brothers and sisters on earth, and for her own salvation. The gifts were hers not because she earned them; they were hers because she was in Christ, and therefore she could claim them as her own, just as anyone in Christ can. These *sancta* are commonly summarized as the Christian faith, the sacraments, and charity.

> "*The experience of fraternal communion leads me to communion with God. Union among us leads to union with God, it leads us to this bond with God who is our Father. ... our faith needs the support of others, especially in difficult moments. If we are united our faith becomes stronger. How beautiful it is to support each other in the wonderful adventure of faith! ... We are all frail, we all have limitations. Nevertheless, in these difficult moments it is necessary to trust in God's help, through child-like prayer, and, at the same time, it is important to find the courage and the humility to open up to others, to ask for help, to ask for a helping hand. How often have we done this and then succeeded in emerging from our difficulty and finding God again! In this communion — communion means common-union — we form a great family, where every member is helped and sustained by the others.*"
>
> — Pope Francis, Wednesday Audience, October 30, 2013

1 German Bishops' Conference, *A Catholic Catechism for Adults: The Church's Confession of Faith*, trans. Stephen Wentworth Arndt (San Francisco: Ignatius Press, 1987), 253.

2 Saint Thérèse of Lisieux, "Act of Oblation to Merciful Love."

The Christian Faith

The faith of Christ is the first and foundational good of salvation that has been handed on generation after generation, beginning with the apostles who first encountered Jesus (Rom 10:17). The Apostles' Creed, which is rooted in the apostles' experience of Christ and recited in the Church's liturgies, serves as one of the first summaries of the Faith. In addition to stating what Christians believe about the Holy Trinity and the Church, the Apostles' Creed also affirms a number of other Church teachings: "the communion of saints, the forgiveness of sins, the resurrection of the body, and life everlasting." This creed, or any other creed approved by the Church, does not exhaust the Faith, for the content of the Faith is also handed on via Sacred Scripture and Sacred Tradition. However, by providing a written list of items held in common, the creed establishes a base from which the communion of believers can be built and strengthened.

The Apostles' Creed

I believe in God,
the Father almighty,
Creator of heaven and earth,
and in Jesus Christ, his only Son, our Lord,
who was conceived by the Holy Spirit,
born of the Virgin Mary,
suffered under Pontius Pilate,
was crucified, died and was buried;
he descended into hell;
on the third day he rose again from the dead;
he ascended into heaven,
and is seated at the right hand of God the Father almighty;
from there he will come to judge the living and the dead.
I believe in the Holy Spirit,
the holy Catholic Church,
the communion of saints,
the forgiveness of sins,
the resurrection of the body,
and life everlasting. Amen.

The Seven Sacraments

If faith is the foundational good of salvation, then the Church's seven sacraments (baptism, confirmation, Eucharist, reconciliation, anointing of the sick, matrimony, and holy orders) could be called the "good" that keeps the disciple on the path of Christ. Hearing the word of God and accepting it into one's life have to be reinforced through perseverance in the grace of Jesus. Therefore, so that faith does not wither and die, the believer must encounter Christ continually, which happens among other ways through the sacraments (which, in turn, enable the disciple to bring Jesus to others). Needless to say, God is not bound by the sacraments and can dispense his grace in any way he wants, but he revealed the sacred mysteries as a privileged means by which Christ offers himself and his grace to the world: through the sacraments, the believer receives Jesus' spirit, his forgiveness, his healing love, a participation in his life of service, and his body and blood. As one participates in and yields himself or herself more deeply to the sacraments, particularly the Mass, he or she is brought into communion with Jesus and all who abide in him (CCC 950).

Charity

Receiving the sacraments well is manifested by the disciple through the indisputable proof of active charity. The Lord says, "This is how all will know that you are my disciples, if you have love for one another" (Jn 13:35). If one is in communion with Jesus and the members of his body, then one is moved to share God's grace with others. Charity is one of the goods of salvation that is given freely because it has been received without cost. And by "charity" the Church does not mean simply a token gift from a person with means to a person with nothing. Rather, "charity" means an offering of one's whole self to one's brothers and sisters for the good of all. A person may have a particular charism to be shared for the benefit of the community; or material possessions like food, clothing, and shelter; or spiritual gifts like mercy, forgiveness, patience, and kindness. Prayer, too, is a gift of charity that should be shared between and among the members of Christ and offered to the world. The main principle to remember is what Saint Paul told the Romans: "None of us lives to himself, and none of us dies to himself" (Rom 14:7). The members of Christ's body are to love one another as Christ loved everyone (Jn 13:34–35).

The full acceptance and practice of the *sancta* builds up the *sancti*, or the communion among holy persons. Since the communion originates in and is sustained by Jesus, who is alive in the communion of the Holy Trinity (with the Father and the Holy Spirit), two consequences are important to keep in mind. First, everyone in communion with Christ is called a "saint," which means "holy one," because he or she shares in the goods of salvation and is destined for heaven (See Eph 1:1; 1 Cor 1:2; Col 1:2). However, the Church also uses "saint" to distinguish a certain group of people among all the holy ones. Second, these holy ones are not limited to the faithful members of the Church on earth. All who have died in Christ are among the communion of saints, too.

"All, indeed, who are of Christ and who have his Spirit form one Church and in Christ cleave together. So it is that the union of the wayfarers with the brethren who sleep in the peace of Christ is in no way interrupted ... " (CCC 954–955).

The Church, grounding its teaching in the words of Christ — "He is not God of the dead but of the living" (Mk 12:27) — has taught always that the communion of the saints is experienced in three states: the earthly pilgrimage, the purification in purgatory, and the glory of heaven.

> *"They devoted themselves to the teaching of the apostles and to the communal life, to the breaking of the bread and to the prayers. Awe came upon everyone, and many wonders and signs were done through the apostles. All who believed were together and had all things in common; they would sell their property and possessions and divide them among all according to each one's need. Every day they devoted themselves to meeting together in the temple area and to breaking bread in their homes. They ate their meals with exultation and sincerity of heart, praising God and enjoying favor with all the people. And every day the Lord added to their number those who were being saved." — Acts 2:42–47*

The saints on earth are in a very different situation than the saints undergoing purification or experiencing glory. The difference is not the simple fact that they have yet to pass through death; it's that the saints on earth still have the possibility of choosing to walk away from Christ. One can hope that a person who has yielded to Christ would remain in Christ always, but people like Judas, who did betray Christ, should keep us from presumption. (For the record, only God knows for certain the ultimate fate of Judas, who could have made a near-death conversion just as the thief on the cross did.)

The German bishops offer some sobering advice for those still walking the path of Christ: the communion of saints is "both a gift and a task."[3] Sharing in the gift means persevering at the task, which is loving God and neighbor according to the way of Jesus. Still, the saints on earth have every reason to be full of hope and joy as they make their journey toward heaven, not only because Jesus said that his way is easy and light as compared to living without him (see Mt 11:30), but also because God "wills everyone to be saved" (1 Tm 2:4). Jesus is the evidence of God's will, and the guarantee of salvation for those who remain in him.

All Souls

For those who remain in Christ and persevere in charity, the passage through death will bring them either to the state of purgatory or the glory of heaven. It should be noted that the people in purgatory and heaven were not necessarily members of the visible Church on earth. Both Jesus (Mt 25:31–46) and the Church (*Lumen Gentium*, 16) make it clear that those who love like Christ, even though they are not conscious of him, are members of his mystical body. Indeed, they responded to the offer of God's grace, albeit without knowing explicitly the source. Members of the Church, however, are charged with making Jesus known through lives of charity.

Ever since the ninth century the Church has celebrated All Souls' Day, when we gather as a community to pray specifically for those who have died. In our prayers for the dead, we remember how they affected our lives. If they were a blessing, we might ask the Lord to bless them. If they caused us pain, we might forgive them and beg the Lord's mercy for them, too. Either way there's a real sense that these people are still a part of our lives. At the very least they remain in our thoughts, and they may even have a real influence on us still. Praying for them allows peace not only for them, but also for ourselves.

Loving like Christ, whether one was a member of the Church or not, does not mean that one did so without errors or even sin. Most people mature in love over a lifetime, and the growth usually comes with a lot of pain and learning from mistakes. However, there is a big difference between those who have given themselves over to sin and those who

3 *A Catholic Catechism for Adults*, p. 253

continue to struggle. As difficult as it may be to imagine, a person may use his or her God-given freedom to reject God. If it is done with full knowledge and full consent, then that person will suffer eternal separation from God. The person who never gives in to sin and tries to change for the better, all the while being attentive to the needs of one's brothers and sisters, may die with the need for further growth. The Church calls this state of purification "purgatory," and the people in this state are those to whom the Church refers as "All Souls."

"Purgatory" is not a state of punishment. It is more accurately seen as a place where God purifies and makes people ready to enjoy full and eternal communion with him. An analogy might be a farmer who has been working in the fields all day. He is sweaty and grimy, and he needs to take a shower before sitting at the dinner table. Purgatory is a loving gift from a father who wants his children to feel completely at home in his presence. Both the Old and New Testaments (2 Macc 12:46; Mt 12:32) affirm the truth of the Church's teaching on purgatory. In fact, the living are told to pray for those in purgatory that their purification may be swift, and the Church takes it for granted that these souls who are near to God offer prayers for their brothers and sisters on earth.

The Saints in Glory

We look forward to the image of heaven described by John in the Book of Revelation:

> I had a vision of a great multitude, which no one could count, from every nation, race, people, and tongue. They stood before the throne and before the Lamb, wearing white robes and holding palm branches in their hands. They cried out in a loud voice: / "Salvation comes from our God, who is seated on the throne, / and from the Lamb ... / Amen. Blessing and glory, wisdom and thanksgiving, / honor, power, and might / be to our God forever and ever. Amen." (7:9–12)

The Church also teaches that there are people who enjoy the glory of heaven now. They include, of course, those who have passed through purgatory, but the Church recognizes that some people yielded themselves so completely to Christ while living on earth that they entered into God's presence immediately after death. First among them is Mary, who never ceased to praise and thank God, her savior (Lk 1:47), and who chose freely every day to accept God's grace and to reject sin. The Church teaches that Mary received the merits of Jesus before the world did (see CCC 490–491).

Mary is unique in her freedom from sin, but many others like John the Baptist and Martha, Maximilian Kolbe and Mother Teresa, responded to God with great generosity and concern for his people. The Church has declared them, as well as hundreds of their brothers and sisters, as saints in the specific sense of those people who not only live in the presence of God but also offer an example of Christian discipleship. These are the very ones the Church celebrates on All

> *"I want to spend my heaven in doing good on earth."* — Saint Thérèse of Lisieux

Saints Day. Like the saints in purgatory, the saints in heaven have not ended their good works, but continue to intercede for those still journeying toward full communion with God.

When those of us still journeying through this life consider the saints, we may fall into an attraction/repulsion dynamic. On the one hand, we admire the saints for their witness and courage: Thomas More opposing King Henry VIII, Edith Stein standing up to the Nazis, Mother Teresa protecting the dignity of the poor, and so many others who chose to honor God even when it was inconvenient or it cost them their lives. On the other hand, the very fervor we find inspiring can also prompt us to keep them at a distance. We tell ourselves: They are a special class of people; they've been given extra grace; I could never be like them. But this is not true. Jesus calls each person to be holy and to honor God above all else, and he gives us the grace we need to do so. The crucial characteristic is desire. What is our deepest desire? Which desires do we feed? The saints detached themselves from possessions in this world — understanding the passing nature of all things — and concentrated their desire on God. This gave them the freedom to be in the world, working for peace, justice, charity, while anticipating heaven. Far from being people with extra special graces, they show what ordinary human beings can do when all their desires are given over to God.

The Church's rich teaching on the Communion of Saints is first and foremost a recognition of the Holy Trinity's deep love for each and every human being. When human beings at the dawn of creation chose to reject God, God did not turn away from them. Rather he chose to forgive them and offer them a way to return to him, all the while respecting the freedom he gave them. The human race, because of God's gift of Christ, has an eternal home and a way to get there. Jesus has provided the goods of salvation through which has been built up a holy people, the visible face of whom is the Church. Moreover, the saints of God persevere in his grace to receive salvation for themselves and to share it with everyone.

— STUDY GUIDE PART 11 ——————————————

The Communion of Saints

STUDY

1. What are the three states of the communion of saints?

2. What is purgatory?

3. What is the difference between All Saints' Day and All Souls' Day?

CONTEMPLATE

1. *A Catholic Catechism for Adults* states the Communion of Saints is "both a gift and a task." In what ways is the Communion of Saints a gift? In what ways is it a task?

2. Do you find it easy or hard to believe in eternal life as promised by Jesus? What is your vision of heaven?

3. Prayer is said to be a gift of charity. How can prayer be a gift of charity? Why is prayer so important to the communal life of the Church?

APPLY

1. We are asked to pray for the souls in purgatory. This week, take a few minutes to remember those in your friends and family who have died this past year.

2. One way to become inspired to holiness is to read the lives of the saints. Who is your patron saint? How can you learn more about your patron?

3. Charity is defined as "an offering of one's whole self to one's brothers and sisters for the good of all." What act of charity, according to this definition, can you perform this week in your family? At your workplace? In the world at large?

PRAYER

Litany of Saints (adapted)

Lord, have mercy.	*Lord, have mercy.*
Christ, have mercy.	*Christ, have mercy.*
Lord, have mercy.	*Lord, have mercy.*
Holy Mary, Mother of God	*Pray for us.*
Holy angels of God	*Pray for us.*
Abraham, our father in faith	*Pray for us.*
David, leader of God's people	*Pray for us.*
All holy patriarchs and prophets	*Pray for us.*
Saint John the Baptist	*Pray for us.*
Saint Joseph	*Pray for us.*
Saint Peter and Saint Paul	*Pray for us.*
Saint Andrew	*Pray for us.*
Saint John	*Pray for us.*
Saint Mary Magdalene	*Pray for us.*
All holy men and women	*Pray for us.*

Shutterstock.com

The Four Last Things

The Catholic Church teaches that there are four last things: death, judgment, hell, and heaven.

As Christians, we know that bringing Jesus' saving acts to bear upon the four last things makes all the difference. Without faith, death can be seen in a merely utilitarian way. Rather than reflecting on it and preparing for it, death becomes something to be forestalled at all costs when life is going well and hastened when life becomes unbearable. Thus life itself becomes simply another possession that one can have or throw away, rather than a gift to be experienced. Moreover, without faith, judgment, hell, and heaven are parts of a grand fairy tale made up by weak people unwilling to face "reality" (see *Evangelium Vitae*, 22).

The Christian, by contrast, sees the four last things precisely as parts of a very real and profoundly meaningful life with God that ex-

PART 12

tends beyond the grave. Indeed, life cannot be understood fully without acknowledging all four. Each of them reflects God's love, mercy, and justice in its own way, as will be explained presently. Given the promises of Jesus — that he would, once and for all, destroy the power of death and open the gates of heaven — every Christian (and everyone searching for the truth) should develop a healthy appreciation of the last things. Death, judgment, hell, and heaven, understood in relation to Christ, must be a part of our overall examination of life. Otherwise, we may miss the blessings such an examination brings. Worse, if God and his truth are shut out willfully, one may suffer the fate of the damned (see *Gaudium et Spes*, 19; *Lumen Gentium*, 16).

"Remember that Jesus Christ, a descendant of David,

was raised from the dead. You can depend on this:

If we have died with him

we shall also live with him;

If we hold out to the end

we shall also reign with him.

But if we deny him he will deny us.

If we are unfaithful he will still remain faithful,

for he cannot deny himself."
— *2 Timothy 2:8, 11–13*

Death

Among the four last things, death is seen by both believers and non-believers as the end of the physical existence human beings enjoy on this earth. But that's where the agreement ends. A faithless view stops at the grave; there's nothing more to consider. The Christian faith, on the other hand, sees death within the context of God's revelation, and there's a lot more to consider.

Based on Scripture and Tradition, and ultimately on Jesus' witness, the Catholic Church recognizes death as the just punishment for the freely chosen sins of human beings.

In the creation stories found in the Book of Genesis, the authors convey the truth that God created a universe that is good, and it is designed according to his laws. God also created human beings to enjoy a relationship with him, which was to be marked not only by fidelity to his will but also by stewardship of his creation and even by the generation of new life. God made human beings in his image, male and female he made them: a communion of persons (reflecting the Trinity) who each enjoyed the gifts of reason and free will. In other words, when making man and woman, God did not desire automatons, but sons and daughters who would choose freely to love each other and their creator.

Human beings, however, chose not to honor their relationship with God, but instead invited death into the world by committing the original sin: rejecting the world as God created it and, instead, asserting themselves as equals to God. Hence the separation from God and the loss of mortal life. Before the first sin, human beings had eternal communion with God as a gift. After sin, an eternity without God is a real possibility.

But it's not the only possibility. God, who gave the gift of freedom to man and woman, is supremely free. He could have responded to sin in a number of ways: scrap everything and start again, or create a new world with new creatures. God responds, however, by honoring the relationship with human beings, even though they did not. And he does so in a just and merciful way that allows both the consequences of sin to follow (namely, death) and the gift of freedom to remain intact.

> *"God did not make death, nor does he rejoice in the destruction of the living. For he fashioned all things that they might have being ... It was the wicked who with hands and words invited death ..."*
> — *Wisdom 1:13–14a, 16a (see also Wisdom 2:23–24)*

In a word, God's response is Jesus. From the moment man and woman sinned, God set into motion his plan of salvation. Human beings could never offer an adequate recompense for their sins, so God offers it for them in the person of Jesus (see Rom 5:17). In effect, God opens the floodgates of his love. The world that had been marred by sin is thoroughly bathed in love through Jesus, "who destroyed death and brought life and immortality to light" (2 Tm 1:10). The sinless one dies for the sinners. What could underscore so powerfully the goodness of creation and, at the same time, the evil of sin? What could convince human beings better — or more gently — that God still desires their eternal happiness than his responding to the evil of sin not with anger, not with bloodlust, but with love?

Jesus has saved the world through his life, death, and resurrection. Human beings now have the opportunity to accept salvation, to turn back to God by receiving his forgiveness and yielding to his will, and, after dying themselves, to enter eternal life.

Understood in the light of Jesus, death takes on a new meaning. It no longer has power over a person who abides in Jesus, for that person has been freed "from the law of sin and death" and received "the spirit of life in Christ Jesus" (Rom 8:2). Saint Paul received this revelation more fully than most and ordered his life upon it: "For to me life is Christ, and death is gain … I am caught between the two. I long to depart this life and be with Christ, [for] that is far better. Yet that I remain [in] the flesh is more necessary for your benefit" (Phil 1:21, 23–24).

Saint Paul grasped the essential meaning of Jesus' saving grace for humankind. While living, he was already united to Jesus, for the kingdom of God was already present in a hidden way (see Lk 17:20–21) and, by his ministry, Paul could bring more people to the Faith as well. As for death, that would only deepen the union with Jesus.

"To rise with Christ, we must die with Christ: we must 'be away from the body and at home with the Lord.' In that 'departure' which is death the soul is separated from the body. It will be reunited with the body on the day of the resurrection of the dead" (CCC 1005).

Therefore, death need not be hastened or forestalled, but can be greeted with serenity when it comes. Passing from this life to the next is simply moving from one way of living in Jesus to another. Saint Paul tried to peel away a bit of the mystery by saying, "That which is corruptible must clothe itself with incorruptibility, and that which is mortal must clothe itself with immortality" (1 Cor 15:53). Indeed, the Scriptures show that Jesus' body had been transformed after the resurrection (cf. Mk 16:12; Lk 24:16; Jn 20:14, 21:4). The meaning is this: for one who remains faithful to Jesus, life is changed, not ended, at death.

Even Christians who hope in the resurrection of Jesus can be deeply affected by death. One must face one's own death and (usually) the deaths of family and friends. Indeed, one may experience great anguish at the thought of dying, just as Jesus did in the Garden of Gethsemane (see Lk 22:39–46). A person also may "weep with those who weep" (Rom 12:15) at the death of a beloved friend, just as Jesus did with Lazarus' family (Jn 11:35). Expressing these deep and real emotions is good and healthy, and it does not mean that one has no faith. Again, Christians may grieve, but not without hope (1 Thess 4:13). They trust in Jesus' words: "Amen, amen, I say to you, you will weep and mourn, while the world rejoices; you will grieve, but your grief will become joy" (Jn 16:20).

Judgment

The Church's teaching on death can have both a comforting and sobering effect. It is comforting to know that life continues, but the fact that one's time on this earth is limited should bring some weightiness to one's decisions. But if death fails to do this, then the Church's teaching on judgment hopefully will: (note that the Church uses "man" in the universal sense, meaning "man and woman") "Each man receives his eternal retribution in his immortal soul at the very moment of his death, in a particular judgment that refers his life to Christ: either entrance into the blessedness of heaven — through a purification or immediately, —or immediate and everlasting damnation" (CCC 1022). There will also be a universal (or last) judgment of the entire universe at the end of time (see CCC 1038–1041).

The basic meaning of the Church's teaching about judgment is that the choices one makes have value — they can be good or bad. Also, God determines the value of one's choices and metes out the appropriate reward or punishment. This teaching tends to evoke two dominant feelings in people: fear and satisfaction.

> "By his salvific work, the only-begotten Son liberates man from sin and death. First of all he blots out from human history the dominion of sin, which took root under the influence of the evil spirit beginning with original sin, and then he gives man the possibility of living in sanctifying grace. In the wake of his victory over sin, he also takes away the dominion of death, by his resurrection beginning the process of the future resurrection of the body. Both are essential conditions of 'eternal life,' that is, of man's definitive happiness in union with God; this means, for the saved, that in the eschatological perspective suffering is totally blotted out." — John Paul II, Salvifici Doloris, 15

Fear, of course, is not a bad feeling to have if one is living a sinful life; it might even prompt one toward conversion. Fear, in the sense of awe, is appropriate too, for God is able to judge everyone and every act in perfect justice and mercy. Only God knows the depths of each person's heart; only he knows the advantages and disadvantages a person had; only he knows the full circumstances of every person's life and every situation. God knows the full truth and will judge accordingly. The only bad kind of fear to have is one that is distrustful of God's judgment, for how could God mistreat the very people he created and saved out of love?

Satisfaction is the other common feeling many people have regarding God's judgment, which is good if by "satisfaction" one means a sense of contentment concerning God's ultimate victory over all evil. A person who is content with God's judgment is able to work diligently for justice on earth without vindictiveness or impatience, knowing that every good effort made at telling the truth, building solidarity, or righting wrongs cooperates with God's victory. A "satisfaction" that hungers for revenge is not a good thing, for it reveals a distrust in God's perfect judgment, which will have the final word (see Rom 12:17–21).

Hell

After we have been judged, we will spend eternity in one of two states: hell or heaven. (Many people think of "hell" and "heaven" as places, but they are more accurately denoted *vis-à-vis* the relationship with God.) Hell is defined by the Church as the "state of definitive self-exclusion from communion with God and the blessed" (CCC 1033). God's judgment in such a case would be to allow the person's choice to take effect, as the *Catechism* relates: "God predestines no one to go to hell; for this, a willful turning away from God (a mortal sin) is necessary, and persistence in it until the end" (1037).

The very mention of "hell" can cause some people to cry "unfair" (placing them in a long tradition going back at least to when Ezekiel was writing; see Ezekiel 18). How could a loving and merciful God allow anyone to suffer eternal damnation? Other people even ignore hell and maintain that Jesus, who loves everyone, will also save everyone. Granted, the thought of hell may be horrifying, but the words of Jesus are clear: "The Son of Man will send his angels, and they will collect out of his kingdom all who cause others to sin and all evildoers. They will throw them into the fiery furnace, where there will be wailing and grinding of teeth" (Mt 13:41–42).

To understand the terrible mystery of hell, the Church directs people to the mystery of freedom, which is a gift human beings have from God. It is a gift that bestows great dignity and enables the person "to initiate and control his own actions" (CCC 1730). But freedom also means that the person is responsible for his or her choices. "The more one does what is good, the freer one becomes. There is no true freedom except in the service of what is good and just. The choice to disobey and do evil is an abuse of freedom and leads to the 'slavery of sin'" (CCC 1733).

Ultimately, saying "no" to hell means saying "yes" to God. Again,

God does not want robots that are forced to love him, but true sons and daughters who choose to love him and their brothers and sisters in freedom. Nevertheless, if they have the freedom to love, then they also must have the freedom not to love. The latter choice leads to hell.

Heaven

Whereas hell is the state of eternal separation from God, heaven is its opposite:

> This perfect life with the Most Holy Trinity — this communion of life and love with the Trinity, with the Virgin Mary, the angels and all the blessed — is called "heaven." Heaven is the ultimate end and fulfillment of the deepest longings, the state of supreme, definitive happiness. (CCC 1024)

And just as a person gets to hell by how he or she lives on earth, so it is with heaven. The crucial difference is that those who choose heaven use their freedom to make every effort at yielding to and accepting God's grace. Another difference is that one can get to hell by oneself, but getting to heaven involves the whole body of Christ, head and members, as Saint Paul reminded the Corinthians: "encourage one another and build one another up" (1 Thes 5:11).

> Purgatory is not one of the four last things because, as a preparation for heaven, it is not eternal. Souls who are in purgatory are being purified by God's mercy so that at the proper time they will be with God in heaven (see CCC 1030–1032).

The essence of heaven is the relationship that human beings enjoy with the Holy Trinity (which includes all the saints), a perfect communion that restores the order God intended when he first created everything. In fact, the Church teaches that, following the Last Judgment, not only humanity but also the entire universe will be transformed into its glorified state (CCC 1060). For human beings this means a reunification with their bodies, now immortal through the grace of the resurrection (see CCC 1052).

Still, to enjoy this communion, human beings must act on God's grace now, here on earth. What this means, practically speaking, is honoring our relationships as God intended. The Book of Genesis suggests "that human life is grounded in three fundamental and closely intertwined relationships: with God, with our neighbor and with the earth itself" (*Laudato Si'*, 66). Sin disrupted these relationships, resulting in separation from God, alienation among neighbors, and disharmony with the earth. God's love in Jesus has made it possible to restore all three.

The choice is before each human person: to love as Christ loves, faithful to the Father, united in the Spirit, and working for the salvation of all. If we join this work now, we will experience its perfection in heaven.

The four last things properly understood in the context of Jesus' life, death, and resurrection need not be so ominous. For example, in what is most likely an apocryphal account, the story is told about Saint Bonaventure eating a meal with his fellow friars. One of them asked Bonaventure what he would do if Jesus were to initiate the Last Judgment at that very moment. And Bonaventure answered, "I'd finish eating my soup." Apocryphal or not, this story captures well the peace, even in the face of death and judgment, of one who abides in Jesus.

— STUDY GUIDE PART 12 ————————————————

The Four Last Things

STUDY

1. What are the four last things?
2. What is death according to both Scripture and Tradition?
3. What is the difference between the particular judgment and the Last Judgment?

CONTEMPLATE

1. Without faith, death becomes something to be forestalled. With faith, death becomes something to be embraced. How does your faith impact your feelings about death?
2. God could have responded to the sin of Adam and Eve in many ways. He chose to honor the relationship with human beings. How do you respond when someone sins against you? How can you continue to honor that relationship?
3. Freedom is a great gift that conveys both dignity and responsibility. Why do you think that God trusted fallible human beings with this great gift?

APPLY

1. "A 'satisfaction' that hungers for revenge is not a good thing, for it reveals a distrust in God's perfect judgment." How can you let go of the desire for revenge in your own life? Can you forgive one person this week?
2. "Saying no to hell means saying yes to God." What is one way that you can reject hell and say yes to God right now?
3. Spend a few minutes thinking about the four last things. What sort of feelings arise as you contemplate your own death and judgment? What changes do you want to make in your life because of this?

PRAYER

Prayer for a Happy Death

Oh, my Lord and Savior, support me in that hour in the strong arms of Thy Sacraments, and by the fresh fragrance of Thy consolations. Let the absolving words be said over me, and the holy oil sign and seal me, and Thy own Body be my food, and Thy Blood my sprinkling; and let my sweet Mother, Mary, breathe on me, and my Angel whisper peace to me, and my glorious saints smile upon me; that, in them all, and through them all, I may receive the gift of perseverance, and die, as I desire to live, in Thy faith, in Thy Church, in Thy service, and in Thy love. Amen.

— *Blessed Cardinal Henry Newman*